The Nort[...]
Traditi[...]

By Pete Jennings

CAPALL BANN PUBLISHING

www.capallbann.co.uk

The Northern Tradition

Previously published as
'The Norse Tradition A Beginner's Guide'

ISBN 186163 1871

First published 1998
This edition first published 2003

Cover design by Paul Mason
Internal illustrations by Dark Moon Designs

Published by:

Capall Bann Publishing
Auton Farm
Milverton
Somerset
TA4 1NE

To all who have taught and influenced me, including
my friends in Odinshof, The Pagan Federation and
my wife Sue.

By the same author:

Pathworking (With Pete Sawyer) (Capall Bann)
Pagan Paths (Ryder 2002)
Mysterious Ipswich (Gruff 2003)
Northern Tradition Information Pack (Pagan Federation 1996)

Contents

Chapter 1

What is the Norse Tradition? - An Introduction

The Norse Tradition is a vibrant, living current within the multitude of spiritual paths of Paganism. It has more than one definition, but it is generally agreed to be the original, natural folk religions of those North Europeans of Teutonic origins. Those traditions come in a multitude of guises, from the temple dwellers at Uppsala, Sweden, to the fiercely independent Icelandic Gothi and Volva roles, and on to the Danish and Saxon settlers and invaders of Britain. Although these forms may be separated by time and distance, they have a common thread of revering nature, and acknowledging a multitude of Goddesses as well as Gods.

Of course, the Celts were doing comparable things in the same geographic area. It can be argued that the Romans classification of tribes as being Celtic or Teutonic was purely arbitrary, and our modern mania for attributing a people to one 'pure' race or another would not have meant much at the time. However, the Celts have developed along a separate path, and are described elsewhere in this series, so let us concentrate on those who share some Teutonic words in their speech, and some common mythology within their culture. It is this rich and colourful mythology, which forms the basis for the Norse Tradition.

The Norse Tradition, sometimes called Odinism (after its chief God Odin), sometimes Northern Tradition (as in

Northern Europe) or Asatru (from words meaning 'a faith in the Gods') is attractive today for many of the same reasons it was followed long ago. It appeals to free thinkers and independent people who want a very direct and straightforward way of expressing their spirituality.

I once described it in a talk as 'Paganism in your face!', and that directness either attracts or repels people, according to their nature. Unlike many other modern Pagan paths it has no formal degree structure, and no universally recognised authoritive figures or revered texts. Such a situation means that the modern practitioner has to think out and do most things for themself. It's evidence is firmly rooted within our culture, and so people with an Anglo Saxon or Danish name and origins are likely to be drawn into a feeling of 'belonging' or 'coming home' to a set of beliefs that gave us so many place names, (such as Grims Dyke) or even the days of the week e.g. Thursday from Thors' day. If you live in the UK it is unlikely that you are not far from a Viking age archae-

A reconstruction of the Sutton Hoo helmet

ological site, such as Jorvik, the old Danish capital at York. If that, or the sight of the treasures from the Anglo Saxon burials at Sutton Hoo, Suffolk (kept in the British Museum) stir you, then maybe a Northern Tradition path might be worth exploring.

Of course, the Vikings ranged far and wide to find new places for trade or raid. They reached a part of North America long before Columbus, and even hauled boats over the mountains to sail down to trade and found a part of Russia. They are well known for their pioneering, adventurous spirit, so you will find people and places bearing elements of Old Norse names all over the world.

Although the modern Norse Tradition shares many features with other Pagan paths, (such as belief in a feminine divine as well as male, and a reverence for nature) there are many aspects that set it apart from Druidry, Wicca etc. Some differences are superficial, such as giving the sun and moon female and male polarity respectively, rather than the more common sun - male / moon - female of Wicca.

Other differences are far more far reaching, in particular the importance Odinists attach to oaths, reputation and keeping ones troth. These will be dealt with in detail in a later chapter, but suffice to say for the moment that these aspects form a very significant part of Heathen thinking. They do have some counterparts in some other traditions, but not to such a highly developed degree.

Incidentally, you may have noticed that I used the word Heathen instead of Pagan just now. Many Odinists prefer this term, although the two words have similar origins; The emperor worshipping Romans dismissively called country dwellers (who still worshipped nature spirits) paganii. 'Heathen' means a dweller of the heath, ie. a person of rural habits, such as worshipping the old Gods. [For a good overview of the range of Pagan paths, see my book *'Pagani Paths'*.

Just as in any other religious path, some people are more committed or involved than others. To some people, simply toasting the Norse Gods occasionally is enough. Others join organisations, form groups (known as hearths), study the mythology, runes and magic or embark on environmental action. One has to decide what one's own commitment is to be, and how far ones own circumstances such as work, finance, home, family etc. will enable you to get involved. Make no mistake, it is a fascinating, lifelong study one can embark upon. It can also be disruptive of one's relationships and attitudes to life, and should probably carry a government health warning!

In exploring the path one will find many contradictions. Because hard archaeological evidence is difficult to find, with many texts fragmentary and enigmatic, people will inevitably put their own interpretations on the facts. Ultimately, there is disagreement, and you must learn to sort out the facts from opinions. For example, you can read dozens of books about runes. Many authors will give the known facts about them, such as their names, shapes, sound and verses relating to them in old poetry. They will then go on to say that they have personally meditated on them, and that for them, the meaning of a certain rune is explained thus... Of course, you can then find another author saying the opposite. Neither is necessarily wrong; the interpretation is right for each of them individually. What you must decide is which is right for you, or to do your own meditation and come up with a third alternative!

I have tried to be as objective as possible in writing this book, but will inevitably be subjective in the opinions and personal prejudices I display along the way, so be aware that you must make choices in how much of it you accept.

Their are different versions of the myths too, which disagree with each other. It is not surprising, as they developed by word of mouth between about 300 AD and 1200 AD, in different languages, conditions and countries thousands of miles apart. That situation isn't unique. After all, the Christian Bible has conflicting elements as well, such as the number of loaves and fishes varying between gospels. What is important is to find the symbolic spiritual truth contained in such stories, not the fiddly details. If you are interested in exploring this path, it is essential to make comparisons between a range of texts, in order to find out what is true for you. There is nobody around to say "do it like this" or "think like that", and that means you must think out ideas, actions and their consequences for yourself.

I believe that any worthwhile spiritual path should effect the follower's daily life, in both thoughts and actions. I also think that it should appeal to the intellect as well as the emotions, and be relevant to the cultural roots and identity of the person involved. So before you immerse yourself in a new way of living, how about some practical work?

Practice

1. Think about yourself. What do you know about your origins? Why not go to a library and find out the meaning and racial origin of your name? Do you feel you belong to the land and race in which you live? Do you feel you wish to have a closer affinity to the wildness of nature, or do you prefer to exercise your spirituality from the comfort of a warm room?

2. What do you want of a new spiritual path? What do you think are the advantages of the Norse Tradition for you personally, and what would you gain from it? Conversely, what would the disadvantages be, and

what personal habits might you have to change to follow this path?

3. Do any of the place names in your locality have Old Norse or Saxon elements within them? The Saxons often used place name endings such as ing (people of), ton (farm) and ham (homestead), whilst the Danes often left their mark in place names finishing in fell, skaw, thwaite, by, beck kirk and gill. Many of these names will be preceded by a personal name e.g. Nacton, (called Nachetuna in 1086) in Suffolk was originally made of the two elements Hnakr and ton. ie. The farmstead of a man called Hnakr. Hnakr is a Norse derived personal name, and ton a Saxon word for a farmstead. Because it is situated in East Anglia, I might guess that this was originally a Danish settlement, since they provided the bulk of Norse influence here, but of course, there was nothing to stop a Saxon calling himself by a Danish name. Inevitably spellings get changed considerably down the years.

Some English place names also contain the names of the old Gods. Look out for places with Grim in the name, such as Grimsby or Grimsdyke. It is an eke or nickname of the god Woden or Odin, in his hooded form. Thundersley in Essex is thought to have come from Thunorsley. Thunor is the Saxon form of Thor the thunder god, leah a Saxon term for a woodland clearing. There are also several 'Harrow hill' type names. It is believed that this denotes a traditional Saxon Pagan altar site, hearg.

Recommended Reading
Pete Jennings - *The Northern Tradition Information Pack* (The Pagan Federation)
Ronald Hutton - *Pagan Religions of the Ancient British Isles* (Oxford)

Prudence Jones & Nigel Pennick - *A History of Pagan Europe* (Routledge)

G. Harvey & C. Hardman - *Paganism Today* (Thorsons)

Kathleen Herbert - *Looking for the Lost Gods of England* (Anglo Saxon)

Teresa Moorey - *Paganism: a beginner's guide* (Hodder & Stoughton)

Dorothy Whitelock - *The Beginnings of English Society* (Pelican)

Kveldulf Gundarsson - *Teutonic Religion* (Llwellyn)

Pete Jenninmgs - *Pagan Paths* (Ryder)

Chapter 2

Back to the Roots

The origins of the Norse mythology and its associated beliefs and religious ideas are hard to pin down. What we do know, is that there was an expansion of tribes out of the area we now know as Germany in the first few centuries AD. They were not a cohesive nation, and different tribes found a range of lands to conquer or occupy. It is said that those Saxons that occupied the area of the Lower Elbe ended up being invited to England in 449 AD as mercenaries by Vortigen (the name translates as `Overking') to repel attacks by Picts and Celts, in the period after the Romans had abandoned Britain. Having achieved that, possibly in collusion with Angles from Angelm and Jutes from Jutland, they decided to stay, and overthrew their employer.

In a decisive battle in Aylesford, Kent, in about 455 AD it was said that the Saxons were victorious under their twin brother leaders, Hengist and Horsa, but that Horsa died of wounds and was buried at the White Horse Stone, which can still be seen today, and is a sacred place to Odinists and others. Interestingly enough, Hengist translates as `stallion', and Horsa as `horse', so maybe they were ceremonial titles, (like Vortigen) rather than their actual names. In any case it was this band of Saxons who introduced a religion of Teutonic origins to England, different to the Celtic and Roman beliefs which preceded them.

The White Horse Stone, Kent

Some tribes went to what became known as Normandy, (providing Britain with a further wave of conquerors centuries after the first arrivals, in 1066.) The bulk of those tribes though occupied what we would now term Scandinavia - cold, often inhospitable lands with only narrow margins around the coast and fjords to sustain life through fishing and farming. Although we tend to think of them as warlike now, most would have been more concerned with surviving through hard work at land or sea.

Their close proximity to the sea encouraged many to venture out as traders far and wide, with cargoes of fur and amber. As their wealth and families increased, there were no new lands for later sons to inherit, as it was the custom for the oldest son to inherit most. There was an important custom of uncles fostering each others sons, to strengthen links between families and to provide a sort of boarding school between cousins. Bonds made in childhood and hospitality received would often mean that the recipients felt a lifelong bond of friendship or troth, very important when it came to defending each other.

They obviously put a great deal of thought into giving and receiving hospitality. There is a text called the Havamal (Sayings of the High One) which is a collection of homilies on how to live, and the greater part of it is concerned with hospitality. The Havamal forms part of a collection of Norse - Icelandic writings known as the Poetic Edda, written down in around 1270 AD but originating from much earlier. The bulk of the 35 poems tell the mythology in verse form, and are preserved in a manuscript called the Codex Regius, which is held in Reykjavik.

The other great literary source of knowledge also comes from Iceland, where many Scandinavians settled after disputes with authority at home. (Some even ventured on from there to the coast of Newfoundland, which they called Vinland, but never stayed to colonise.) This second book is called the Prose Edda, and was written by Snorri Sturluson in the early 13th century. Like the Poetic Edda, it was written in a society with Christian influences, but it contains the sources and details of many of the Norse myths we know today. It was written under the pretext of being information for poets on alliteration, form and kenning, maybe the only way such a text could have been published at the time. Kenning incidentally is the art of finding other more poetic ways of saying things e.g. The sea becomes the fishes bath.

The fact that Iceland is our major source of written information is perhaps significant. Iceland was one of the last countries in our corner of the world to be officially converted to Christianity, in 999 or 1000 AD. Even then, the law permitted individuals to sacrifice and worship the old Gods in the privacy of their own homes, as well as eating horseflesh, (a part of staple diet for some Icelanders at that time which was disapproved of by Christians.) This gave the

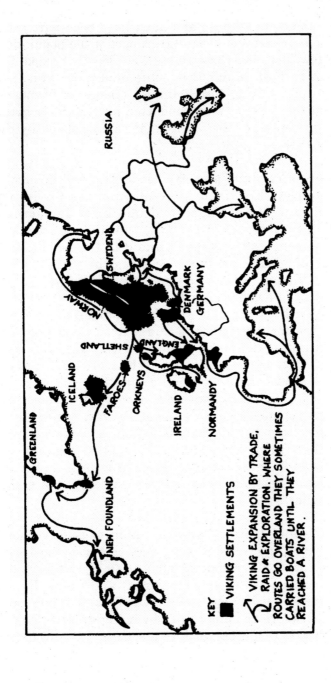

Map showing a selection of migrations and invasions

17

country a unique dual faith, and must have been partly due at least from pressure of a significant part of the population. Within a few lifetimes, those rights were legally eroded, but Asatru was revived as an official state dual religion in 1973 due to the work of Sveinbjorn Beinteinsson and his friends. It means that today, a wedding conducted by a gothi or gytha (priest or priestess) of the old religion is recognised by the authorities there.

Women having rights to property, leadership and divorce, a legal system with a fixed table of damages for injury sustained, and the village governed by a democratic assembly of freemen called a Thing, which gives origins to other parliaments such as the Tynwald in the Isle of Man; Does this sound like the barbaric races the monks wrote about? The Vikings did not do much writing, so we are left mainly with the heavily biased accounts of those that they attacked. As the centres of wealth, monasteries were the obvious target for those came to raid instead of trade in 793 AD at Lindisfarne, and elsewhere in the following two centuries. The Saxon, Celts and Picts all kept slaves, slaughtered prisoners of war, and committed various other atrocities. The Viking raiders were no better or worse, but were written about in a more negative way. Incidentally, Viking refers to a mixed group of Scandinavian races who went raiding. To go a-viking was to go a-pirating, and the warriors could have been Danes, Jutes, Angles or any of the other tribes from that region. Saxon writers often called them all Danes.

Despite the bloodthirsty way in which they have been portrayed since, the Norse peoples were very concerned with poetry and other finer things, such as fine jewellery, and playing board games such as hnefatafl and chess. It was thought (and still is by most modern Odinists) that one could achieve a measure of immortality by doing great things in ones life, which would be put into a song by a skald (poet).

The more spectacular the events and thus the song, the longer it would be sung after ones death, providing a way of being remembered. In the early period of Norse beliefs, there was a fatalistic idea of ones life span being predetermined by the Norns, the three Wyrd sisters. One would not die until your time was up, so you might as well live courageously and honourably. It is possible that belief in heavens such as the warriors Asgard or the families Sessrunner Hall (under the protection of Freyja) did not come into consciousness until the later Viking and Saxon periods.

Once they did have beliefs about an afterlife, and of a figure hanging on a tree wounded by a spear (Odin in his quest for the runes) those Norse & Saxon of Pagan beliefs must have been more easily converted to Christianity, although how genuine it was for people ordered to do so by their kings (sometimes at the point of a sword) is doubtful. Certainly King Raedwald of East Anglia, (buried at Sutton Hoo) accepted baptism from the King of Kent's priest possibly as an act of political necessity, but set up the Christian altar alongside three heathen ones. His spectacular ship burial in around 625 AD was certainly a demonstrably Pagan affair. I suppose that if you already have several gods and goddesses, one extra doesn't seem important in that context. Although the Danes martyred King Edmund for his faith in 869 AD, for the most part they seemed content to let conquered peoples continue with their original religion, and frequently added it to their own, in a sense that they were more accepting of others beliefs than Christianity was of theirs. Within about 100 years of killing King Edmund the Danes were striking coins at his burial place (Bury St. Edmunds) with his saintly image on them.

Olaf Tryggvasson on the other hand took a much less tolerant line. He was a Pagan when he won the Battle of Maldon in 991 (described in an old English poem of that name) and returned again to raid London and extract more Danegeld ransom money with Svein Forkbeard in 994. That winter, he stayed on at the Saxons expense, and was converted to Christianity. The following year when he began a five year reign as King of Norway, he started a programme of very forced conversion, which spread to its dominions such as Iceland.

The Norse did not leave too much contemporary writing, and being mainly wooden, most of their buildings have disappeared. We do have a few reports about them from foreigners such as the Roman Tacitus, who wrote about the Teutonic tribes rune casting, and from the Saxons they attacked. What we are left with is some extensive burial sites. Norse leaders were often buried in mounds, and stones with runic inscriptions erected. In many places (such as Lindholm Hoje, Jutland, Denmark) the boat shaped grave outlines of less important folk are marked out in plain stones. The ship motif is obviously an important symbol to them. It features in their art and stories, and their close proximity to the sea in their settlements meant that it was important for them to be successful sailors, which they were. They were not content to rely on similar ship designs to everyone else, but developed the fastest, most efficient craft of their time. It is this adventurous spirit that shines through as the embodiment of their attitude - a forward looking, hardy and independent people. It is that same spirit that the Norse tradition tries to live by today - conscious of its great past history, but wanting to be accepted by the rest of the world on its own terms.

Practice

1. Why not try and see some real Viking or Saxon artefacts for yourself? You could visit a local museum, or better still visit the Anglo Saxon section of the British Museum, Gt. Russell St., London where treasures from Sutton Hoo and elsewhere are kept.

(Tel. 0171 636 1555). The Jorvik Centre Coppergate, York, (Tel. 01904 643211) is built over an archaeological dig of the old Viking city, and has some superb exhibits including reconstructed scenes of the past, including sounds and smells! At the Vikingar Viking Heritage Centre, Barfields, Greenock Rd., Largs, Scotland KA30 8QL there are films, tableaux and Viking God heads to be seen. (Tel. 01475 689777.) Further afield, you might like to visit the runic stones found in parts of Sweden and elsewhere, or the Viking Ship Museum in Oslo, Sweden. There you can see both the Gokstad and Oseberg burial ships, together with their associated grave goods such as the Oseberg wagon.

2. The Norse mythology is too vast to even begin to give you a taste of it in a book such as this. I strongly advise you to get hold of a good authoritive version of some of the stories, such as the one by Crossley - Holland. You can read them at many levels - as exciting stories, as disguised histories or as the carriers of spiritual truths. It is good to compare more than one translation of the stories, so as to avoid being influenced by any individual authors opinions and interpretations. Beware though of Wagner's Ring Cycle opera! He took some mythological elements, added to them, changing and adding characters to make an epic work but a confusing menu of red herrings for the novice to swallow.

Recommended Reading
Kevin Crossley-Holland - *The Norse Myths* (Penguin) - *Axe Age, Wolf Age* (Faber & Faber)
Snorri Sturluson (trans. J. Young) - *The Prose Edda* (University of California)
Anon. (trans. C. Larrington) - *The Poetic Edda* (Oxford)

Angela Care Evans - *The Sutton Hoo Ship Burial* (British Museum)

Hilda R. Ellis Davidson - *Gods & myths of Northern Europe* (Pelican)

Gwyn Jones - *A History of the Vikings* (Oxford University)

Bryan Branston - *Lost Gods of England / Gods and Heroes from Viking Mythology* (Book Club Associates)

Magnus Magnusson - *Hammer of the North* (Book Club Associates) *The Viking expansion Westwards / Iceland Saga / The Vikings* (all Bodley Head) *The Vinland Sagas* (Penguin)

Clive Barrett - *The Viking Gods* (Aquarian)

Anon. trans. Bill Griffiths - *The Battle of Maldon* (Anglo Saxon)

John Grant - *Viking Mythology* (Quintet)

David Wilson - *The Vikings and their origins* (Thames & Hudson)

James Graham Campbell - *The Viking World* (Windward)

Sir Frank Stenton - *Anglo Saxon England* (Clarendon)

Alby Stone - *Ymir's Flesh: North European Creation Mythologies* (Capall Bann)

Chapter 3

Basic Beliefs

Historically, the beliefs of the Norse and Saxon peoples varied greatly, both between different geographic areas, and at different times between the golden age of their first flowering, about 300 AD to 1000 AD. A villager in 4th century Denmark may only have had three gods and goddesses. Because of poor communications, they may have been very different to the deities of a village only a few miles away. Certainly, he wouldn't have known the whole range of stories which have been published today, although he might have known a few that we know have since been lost. Going back to that village a few centuries later, we might find entirely different deities being acknowledged, as ideas spread from elsewhere, or the needs of the community turned from protecting crops to ships. People tend to relate to the gods and goddesses they need, and the same applies today.

One will find a huge variety of beliefs between followers of our tradition today. None of them are necessarily wrong, as they are each interpreting what is right and relevant within their own lives. Just as in the past, some will hold dear to one particular set of gods and goddesses. Some will be content in simple beliefs, others want to know the history and reasoning behind them. A few will be more involved than others, and some will use their beliefs to work magic. Many will be content to just celebrate and acknowledge their faith either at each full moon or on specific festival days.

Hopefully by now you will have read some of the Norse mythology, and how it has two families of deities, the Aesir and Vanir. There are well over a hundred Norse deity names known, excluding the multitude of eke names (nicknames) attached to some gods, as I have shown in the accompanying table. We do not know so much about the Vanir, or so many of their names, but they do all appear to be an older family of nature gods, which at some stage battled with the incoming Aesir. Although some Aesir seem to have natural associations, such as Thor / Thunor with thunder, most seem to be more connected with civilisation e.g. His wife Sifs golden hair representing the golden corn of agriculture, which is cut off in mischief by Loki, who has to replace it with pure spun gold.

One should beware of seeing Gods by single attributes, as many are quite complex. e.g. Thor/ Thunor, one of the main three Gods worshipped together with Odin and Frey is sometimes simply seen as a muscular guardian, hitting the *etin* (giant) enemies of Asgard. However, in one myth he engages a dwarf in a lengthy conversation to trick him into being there when the sun arises, which turns the dwarf to stone. This very different tactic shows a more intellectual side to our hero.

At the end of the war, hostages were exchanged, with the Vanir sea god Njord coming to live with the Aesir with his son and daughter Frey and Freyja. Their names translate as Lord and Lady, the names with which many witches address their deities. It is interesting (and highly contentious) to speculate on that connection with them! Freyja is sometimes confused with Frigga, but they are very different characters. Whilst Frigga is associated with marriage and motherhood, Freyja takes many lovers. This includes four dwarves, from whom she obtains the Brisingen necklace. No one can say for sure what the magical significance of the necklace was, but they are a feature of many goddesses over a long period in various parts of the world. It is said that as well as leading the Valkyries who choose the best slain warriors for Valhalla, Freyja taught Odin, the chief Aesir God, the Vanir art of *seidr* magic, which was considered to be very different to the Aesir galdr magic.

He in turn taught it to others, but it was considered somehow unmanly. Odin has a huge range of attributes and names, connected with wind, war, masks, death etc. but as the All Father God he is in constant pursuit of more knowledge and wisdom. He sacrifices one eye to gain it at Mimirs well, as well as hanging from Yggdrassil wounded by his own spear Gungnir to gain the runes. He has two ravens, Huggin & Munnin (Thought & Memory) who survey the world for him, and two wolves Freki & Geri (Greedyguts & Gobbler) who accompany him on some journeys. He also has a lightning fast eight legged horse called Sleipnir.

Odin had not always been the chief god, Tyr (or Tiw) appearing to have previously taken that role. Tyr takes a crucial role in the binding of the monstrous Fenris wolf, which is in danger of destroying the Gods if it cannot be subdued. A succession of cunning bonds is offered to it to test its strength, but it will not try the most effective without the surety of a hand placed in its mouth. Tyr is the only one courageous enough to do this, knowing that he will lose it when the Gods refuse to untie it again. Thus the one handed God Tyr symbolises challenge, bravery and sacrifice.

Fenris was one of the terrible offspring of Loki, who also produced the Jormungand world serpent, Hel the guardian of the dead and Sleipnir, Odins 8 legged horse. Loki starts as a trickster, often having to get the Gods out of scrapes which he has got them into, such as the losing of the Goddess Iduns apples which keep the deities young. Later, he gets more malevolent as tales develop, culminating in him causing the death of the pure sun God Balder by means of a mistletoe dart. After some prophetic dreams, Balders mother Frigga (wife of Odin, Goddess of housewives and fertility) had got all the plants to swear an oath not to harm him, but had missed out the mistletoe. The other Gods had a game throwing missiles at Balder, and watching them bounce off. Loki asks Hoder, Balders blind brother to join in, giving him the fateful dart and guiding him. For this act, and for showing no remorse afterwards, he is bound to a rock with a venom dripping snake above his head. His wife Sigyn undertakes to catch the poison in a bowl, but has to leave him to scream and shake the world to earthquakes when she empties it. He is due to break free at Ragnarok, the final battle between the deities and forces of evil, which will be signaled by the blasts from a huge horn belonging to Heimdall, guardian of the Bifrost rainbow bridge.

It is stated in one text that the goddesses are equal in status to the gods, but unfortunately, there are far fewer individual stories about them. What we can tell from the stories is that unlike many other mythological tales, they have minds and characters of their own, independent of the male gods. This reflects the high position accorded a woman in Norse society, where she was the keeper of the household and its keys, and had property and divorce rights. This is also reflected in the Norse tradition today, where men and women are seen as equals, with either having the ability to set up and govern a hearth group. In many other goddess orientated Pagan paths the woman is put in an ascendant position, such as witches covens traditionally run by a High Priestess.

Many of the stories told about the gods and goddesses revolve around the constant threat to their world and family from the giants. Many of the giant names translate into terms for elemental natural forces, such as whirlpool, mountain, waterfall etc. So it would seem that the gods are battling with nature itself. The anachronism for me is that if you go back to the creation myths, the early gods are often born of part giant parentage. Thus they are fighting a war against part of themselves. I will return to this them in a little while.

All Aesir unless annotated V for Vanir. No pseudonyms used and the gender is not always constant. Names in small type in first three columns indicate non-deity i.e. Giant (Etin) human or dwarf. Att. = Attendant of.

NB. It is always possible that some of the lesser names are *eke* names (nicknames) for deities featured elsewhere in the chart. Some deities such as Odin have many names or titles. The etymology of words is fraught with conjecture and debate and research is ongoing.

Name	Gender	Partner	Children	Attributes
AEGIR	m	RAN	9 Waves f	Sea
ALI	m			Marksman (also known as Vali)
ANNAR	m	NOTT	ERDA f	The other one
AUD	m			Prosperity
BALDER	m	NANNA	FORSETI m	Purity/light
BJORT	f			Beautiful
BLEIK	f			Blond one
BLID	f			Friendly one
BRAGI	m	IDUN		Poetry. Runes carved on tongue
BURI	m		BURR m	Producer
BURR	m	Bestla	ODIN m VILI m VE m	Son
BIL	f			Moment. Weaving
DAG	m	THORA		Day
DELLINGER	m	NOTT	DAG m	Dawn–third husband
EIRA	f			Medicine att. of Frigga
ERCE	f			Earth
ERDA	f			
FJORGYN	f		ODIN &THOR	Earth
FORSETI	m			Chairman Justice

Name	Gender	Partner	Children	Attributes
FREY (V) (or INGVI FREY)	m	Freygerda	Frodi m	Lord. Fertility Aesir Hostage
FREYIA (V)	f	OD ODIN Ottar Alfrigg Dvalin Berling Grerr	GERSEMI f HNOSS f	Lady. Sex, war. Frequently confused with Frigga. Last 4 dwarf lovers made Brisingen necklace
FRIGGA	f	ODIN	BALDER m	Fertility, house wives (MENGLAD)
FRITH	f			Pretty
FULLA	f			Full haired. Att. of FRIGGA
GEFION	f			Virgins. Att. of FRIGGA
GERSEMI	f			
GLENR	m	SOL		Opening in cloud
GNA	f			Att. of FRIGGA
HEIMDALL	m	Many lovers	3 Races	Guardian of Bifrost rainbow bridge
HEL	f	ULL		Guardian of Hel
HELGI	m	GUDRUN		
HERMOD	m			ODIN's messenger
HLER	m			Early sea God
HLIN	f			Consolation Att. of FRIGGA
HNOSS	f			Treasure
HODER	m			Blind son of Odin – killed Balder with Loki
HOENIR	m			Early God gave emotion and senses Bro. ODIN and LOKI

Table of Norse deities (cont.)

Name	Gender	Partner	Children	Attributes
HONIR	m			Indecisiveness
IDUN	f	BRAGI Ivuld		Spring. Immortal apples.
ING (V)	m			East Danes
IRPA	f			Dark Brown
KARI	m			Early God of Air
KVASIR (V)	m			Wisdom, mead
LODUR	m			Early God gave blood
LOFN	f			Eases path of true and illicit love
LOKI	m	SIGYN Thokk Angrboda	Sleipnir HEL f Fenrir Jormungland NARVI m VALI m	Lies, tricks evil, fire. After causing death of BALDER bound until Ragnarok
MAGNI	m			Might
MIMIR	m			His head is the oracle of a Well of Wisdom
MODI	m			Wrath
NAGLFARI	m	NOTT	AUD m	
NANNA	f	BALDER		
NARVI	m			Guts bind LOKI
NERTHUS (V)	f	NJORD	FREY m FREYJA f	Sea
NIGHT	f		NARVI m	Night
NJORD (V)	m	NERTHUS Skaldi	FREYJA f FREY m	Sea
NORNS;				Fates:
SKULD	f			Being
URD	f			Fate
VERDANDI	f			Necessity

Name	Gender	Partner	Children	Attributes
NOTT	f	NAGLFARI ANNAR DELLINGER	AUD m ERDA f DAG m	Night
OD	m	FREYJA	HNOSS f GERSEMI f	Left FREYJA
ODIN	m	FJORGYN FRIGGA RIND SAGA Grid	THOR m BALDER m HODER m TYR m BRAGI m HEIMDALL m ULL m VIDAR m HERMOD m VALI m SIGI m	Chief God – the Allfather. Runes and Wind. Many eke names. Ravens Hugin and Mugin (Thought/Memory) Wolves Freki and Geri. (Greedyguts and Gobbler) Spear Gugnir
OSTARA	f			Spring
RAN	f	AEGIR (wife/sister)	9 Wave maidens	Sea. Net to pull down sailors.
RIND	f	ODIN	VALI m	Frozen soil
SAGA	f	ODIN		Stories
SATAERE	m			Agriculture
SIF	f	THOR ODIN	ULL m	Golden corn hair ULL by ODIN
SIGI	m			Victor
SIGURD	m	BRUNHILD GUDRUN		
SIGYN	f	LOKI	NARVE m VALI m	Empties cup of poison
SKADI	f	NJORD ULLR	FREY m FREYJA f	Snowshoes
SKALDI	f	ODIN		Poetry
SKIRNIR	f			Shining one
SJOFN	f			Human passion
SNOTRA	f			Virtue. Att. of Frigga

Name	Gender	Partner	Children	Attributes
SOL	f	GLENR		Sun
SUMAR	m			Summer
SVASID	m		SUMAR m	Gentility
SYN	f			Trials, denial
THOR	m	SIF Iarnsaxa	MAGNI m MODI m	Thunder, law, Fertility. Has Hammer Mjollnir, Grid's belt and gauntlets of strength. His chariot is pulled by goats Tanngnost and Tanngrisni
TYR	m			War/ Courage. Chief before Odin. Lost hand to Fenris Wolf
ULLR	m	SKADI FRIGGA		Winter, archery.
VALI	m			Avenges Balder. Son of ODIN/RIND
VALI	m			Turned wolf to kill Narve (Son of LOKI)
VALKYRIES	f	– see list at end		Select slain for Valhalla
VARA	f			Beloved, Oaths.
VASUD	m		VINDSVAL m	Unfriendly
VE	m	FRIGGA		Early God – Brother of VILI
VIDAR	m			Will slay Fenris and survive Ragnarok
VILI	m	FRIGGA		Early God Brother of VE
VINDSVAL	m		WINTER m	Cold wind

The table of Norse deities (cont.)

Name	Gender	Partner	Children	Attributes
VJOFN	f			Conciliation Att. FRIGGA
VOR	f			Careful One Faith. Knowledge of future.
WINTER	m			Winter
WYRD	f		NORNS f	Early Goddess

VALKYRIES are led by Freyja in selecting the slain.

Name	Gender	Partner	Children	Attributes
ALVIT	f	Son of King Nidud		Allwise
BRUNHILD	f	SIGURD GUTTORM	Sigdrifa	Victory giver
GEIDRIFIL	f			Spear flinger
GEIRAHOD	f			Battle
GEIRAVOR	f			Spear goddess
GOLL	f			Screaming/fight
GONDUL	f			Magic animal
GUDRUN	f	HELGI SIGURD ATLI		
GUNN	f			Battle
GYNRITHIA	f			
HERFJOTUR	f			Army fetterer
HERYA	f			Devastate
HILDR	f			Battle
HJALMTHIMUL	f			Helmet clatterer
HLOKK	f			Shrieking
HRIST	f			Shaker
KARA	f			Stormy
MIST	f			Mist
NIPT	f			Sister
OLRUN	f	Son of King Nidud		Beer rune

Name	Gender	Partner	Children	Attributes
RADGRID	f			Bossy
RANDGRID	f			Shield destroyer
REGINLIEF	f			Daughter of Gods
ROTA	f			
RUSILA	f			Red haired
SANNGRINDR	f			Very violent
SHAKER	f			Mead bringer to ODIN
SIGRUN	f			
SKALMOLD	f			Sword time
SKEGGOLD	f			Battle axe
SKOGULL	f			Mead bringer to ODIN
SKULD	f			Blame
STICLA	f			
SVANHVIT	f	Son of King Nidud		Swanwhite
SVAVA	f			Put to sleep
SVEID	f			Noise
THOGN	f			Silence
THRIMA	f			Fight
THRUD	f			Power woman

There are also many dwarf and giant names recorded. Most of the giant names translate into uncomplimentary terms e.g. sooty face, hairy hands etc., but many others have meaning in various natural forces such as fire, snowdrift etc. Similarly, many of the place and river names translate into decriptions, e.g. Hel's underworld hall Eljuthnir means 'the one dampened by rain'.

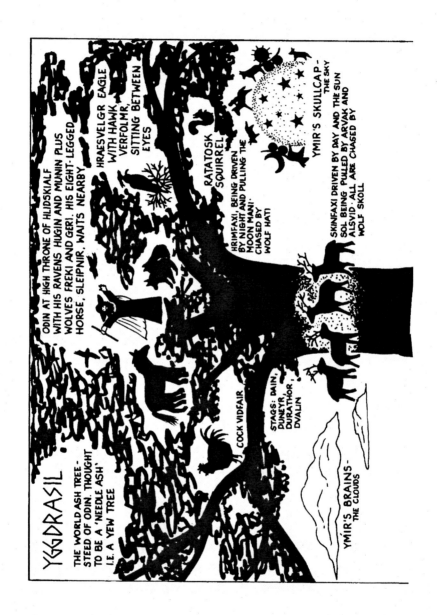

34

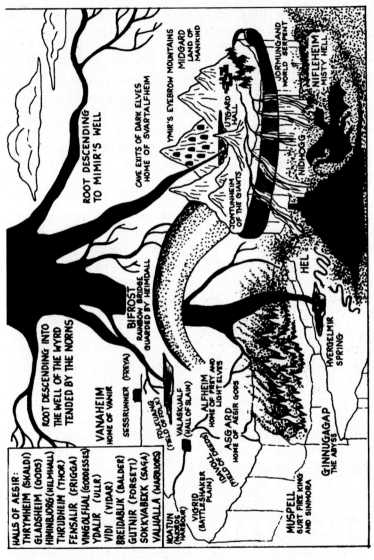

Yggdrasil – The World of Ash Tree, now believed to be a 'needle ash' i.e. yew

The tales take place around the nine worlds contained within the world ash tree Yggdrassil (Meaning steed of the terrible one, Odin.) A writer I respect, Nigel Pennick suggests that Yggdrassil may actually be a yew. Apparently, yews were sometimes called 'needle ash' and it would make sense to have a tree that is evergreen, has a number of trunks, and which exude narcotic vapours. It would certainly provide a dangerous way to go on a shamanic journey, such as Odins self sacrifice, hanging for nine nights, wounded by his own spear to gain the secret of the runes. In the stories, various forces work for and against the continuity of the nine worlds, but eventually, Raganarok, the final battle between good and evil is foretold, in which both sides are destroyed, and a handful of survivors make a fresh start.

There are several ways in which we can regard the stories today. Firstly, as cracking adventure yarns. Secondly, as the carriers of esoteric knowledge or spiritual truths. Thirdly, we might perceive some of them as distorted or exaggerated versions of real historical events. I think there is an element of all those. The way we might regard the stories is probably closely akin as to how we regard the gods and goddesses portrayed within them.

We can perceive the gods and goddesses as supernatural forces, that have always been in existence. Alternatively, we could say that they are part of a group imagination and consciousness. e.g. A tribe is worried about the success of its crops, so makes a goddess to protect them. By talking to her, acknowledging to each other she exists, she eventually does exist, for as long as people believe in her.

If that sounds far fetched, lets take a modern belief - the wind. Our Norse forefathers told of a giant eagle, Hraesvelgr, flapping his wings to cause the wind. Nowadays, meteorologists explain it by telling us about barometric pressure differences. The point is, that both then and now, we believe in a wind, without ever being able to see it. We can see its effects, such as leaves blowing along the ground, but until someone else in the future comes up with another more convincing explanation, people have a general belief in a phenomenon called the wind, just as they once had a belief in a flat earth. The belief in wind is one held in common with most other people. Therefore, the wind exists. In that same way, a god or goddess artificially created by a people will exist for as long as it is believed in. It can even change, and take on a life of its own as successive generations interpret it in slightly different ways.

Illustration of Odin

There is yet another option in how we regard our deities. Modern psychological thinking tells us how our minds are a collection of contradictory ideas. One part may say 'eat the chocolate, it is tasty.' Another says 'no, it is bad for you and will make you fat and unattractive.' A third says 'who cares?' We can align our deities (or if you prefer, Jungian archetypes) as different personality traits and drives. Thus we might consider it is Loki, the mischievous god tempting us with the chocolate, Balder the pure telling us to look after our body and Odin suggesting that we think independently. Going back to the idea I presented about gods being of part giant parentage, one could think of the bar of chocolate as a giant, made of fat that is much like human or god fat! At a deep level, I think of my gods as aspects of my various personality traits, but on a daily basis it is easier to think of them as beings with individual characters and features, rather than some abstract psychological concept, and I speak as someone with four years of formal psychological training!

Many Odinists have a very direct and personal relationship with their gods and goddesses that does not need to be intellectualised, and there is nothing wrong with a simple faith. That relationship tends to be very straightforward. The myths show us that the gods are more likely to admire a proud and independent spirit who acts honourably and doesn't make excuses for not achieving aims, than a sycophant who tries to suck up to them. They require respect, but not abject humility. In most cases in the myths, if they notice humans at all, they behave in a fairly arbitrary fashion towards them, and are as likely to decide the outcome of a battle on the persuasion of a goddess lover rather than fervent sacrifice and prayer from below.

There is also another central set of ideas very important in understanding the beliefs of both the old and modern Northern tradition. Many believe in a concept termed wyrd. This can be pictured as an infinite spiders web of threads, all inter connected to each other. Some of those threads are peoples lives, which are controlled by the Norns or Wyrd sisters, who are Urd, Verdandi and Skuld,which translate as Fate, Necessity and Being. Thus, every action we take, trembles along the web, and effects others. There is also an idea of orlog, which refers to a Person's individual fate being fixed. Thus, one cannot change for instance the date of ones death, but one can alter the way at which it arrives. This belief may lead to a stoic attitude - if I am fated to die in battle today, I might as well do it bravely, (and maybe get picked by the Valkyries to go to the warrior heaven Asgard) since I'm going to die anyway, whether I fight bravely or try to run away. There is historical evidence to of Icelandic settlers letting the Gods of chance decide where they actually lived, by casting carved wooden high seat posts from their old home or temple overboard as they approached land. Where they beached was where they chose to live. This was done by Thorolfur Mostrarskeggi in 884 (in the Eyrbyggja Saga) and previously to that by one of the earliest settlers, Ingolfur Arnarson ten years earlier.

You will have already read in chapter 2 about how important family and tribal ties were. This is carried forward to today, and true Norse tradition Pagans tend to be extremely loyal to their Hearth group, long after it has dispersed, and seeded newer groupings. This especially applies to their original leaders. In this they parallel the loyalty expected of a man to his eorlderman, gothi or other leader in times past. It was considered a severe punishment for a leader to disown a member of his tribal group, because they would no longer have their lord's protection against theft, murder or slavery from outsiders.

There is a tradition of taking oaths on either a ring or sword within our tradition, (before the goddess of oaths,Vara) going back to those times. These oaths are taken extremely seriously, and in the Viking age, an oath breaker was often regarded as worse than a murderer. So a Hearth for example that has taken an oath to protect each other, regards that as an ongoing responsibility regardless of what other circumstances or personal disputes might prevail. This feeling of mutual protection (whether done under oath or just by belonging to the same group) is known as 'Troth', and is a vital component of Norse tradition, which tends to set it apart from some other Pagan traditions. I will give you an example how some of these things work out in practice from my own life.

A year or two ago, I was a guest with my wife at a large Pagan gathering which was taken over by half a dozen knife wielding neo nazi thugs. We stood up to them, and had our lives threatened. We both felt it was our duty to confront their desecration of the ritual, were aware that we were in danger but did not ask that anyone else put themselves on the line. We just suggested that people who didn't approve left. From the far side of the circle of about a hundred people, a lady walked directly across and stood at my wife's other shoulder. I don't think the thugs had ever been confronted with two such formidably strong women before (which I now refer to as the Valkyrie contingent!) and eventually backed down. Afterwards, a friend said how brave, yet foolhardy the lady was. She replied that she had no choice in the matter. As an ex member of our Hearth (disbanded when we moved away) she was still troth with us, despite a fairly major disagreement I had with her before the split. I think that is a very good modern example of someone keeping their troth.

Practice

1. In the example given above, how do you think you would have reacted, if you had been troth with me? Do you think that there are some ideals worth dying for?

2. What things might you want to consider before you take a personally binding oath?

3. We used magic to protect ourselves, which would seem to have been successful. The main aggressor was eventually repelled by magically sending all his hate back at him. Do you think that was ethically correct, or

should we have let fate (wyrd) catch up with him in its own good time?

Recommended Reading
Anon. (trans. John Porter) *Beowulf,* Text & Translation (Anglo Saxon)
Sam Newton - *The Origins of Beowulf* (Boydell & Brewer)
Anon. (trans. G.A.Hight) *The Saga of Grettir the Strong* (Everyman)
Anon. (trans. Palsson & Edwards) - *Orkneyinga Saga -Egils Saga* (both Penguin)
Anon. (trans. Gwyn Jones) - *Eirik the Red & other Icelandic Sagas* (Oxford)
Judith Jesch - *Women in the Viking Age* (Boydell)
Magnusson & Palsom - *The Vinland Sagas* (Harmondsworth)
G. Harvey & C Hardman - *Paganism Today* (Thorsons)
Brian Bates - *The Wisdom of the Wyrd* (Rider)
Nicholas Size - *Shelagh of Eskdale* (Frederick Warne)
H.A. Guerber - *Myths of the Norsemen* (Harrap)

Chapter 4

The Runes

Runes are at their simplest, marks scratched or written to convey an idea, and yet the study of them can take place over the whole of one's life. This is such a vast and involved subject that I can only provide a basic introduction to it here. I have some strong feelings about the runes, and am sometimes annoyed that they have been misused so often by so many people over the years. Let me start at the beginning though, with their origins.

Within the mythology, Odin hangs for nine days and nights from the world ash Yggdrassil, self wounded by his own spear (gugnir), as it was said a sacrifice of himself to himself. At the end of the of the ordeal, he snatches the knowledge of the runes from the void, which I personally interpret as Ginnugagap.However it is looked upon, there is a clear spiritual message there - the runes require sacrifices of those who wish to know them, and they are a serious pursuit, not some frivolous fortune telling game. They are also firmly placed within Norse mythology, and no others, so it would seem inappropriate for people following other religious paths to mess about with them. After all, other mythologies have their own equivalents, such as the Celtic Druids' ogham script.

Historically, it is difficult to place the exact origins of the runes. For example, one character, gyfu is a simple diagonal cross. Just because someone carved a cross onto a rock in 300 BC doesn't mean that people were calling them or using them as a runic alphabet. In fact, strings of such symbols do not seem to have been associated together for at least another 600 years, in about 300 AD.

There is some argument as to whether they grew up independently, or were part influenced by other alphabets. It is perfectly possible for two people to invent similar simple marks without having seen the others work. The early runes were made of straight lines, which is very important if you want to carve them into rock, wood or metal with crude tools. It was not until more sophisticated writing methods came along that some of the forms became more rounded. It appears that the earliest alphabet of these runes had 24 characters. Just as alphabet is made up of the first letters alpha, beta, runic alphabets are called futhorks or futharks, after the sound of their first six characters. From that Elder Futhark, as it is known, came many others, as the language and living conditions altered. (Even today we have to invent new words for new situations, such as the computer term modem.) For example, there is an Anglo Saxon futhork of only 18 runes, but at the same time another one in Northumbria of 32 runes. There are other variations by geographic area (Iceland, Frisia etc.) and by time period. The language and the way it was written developed over the 700 years odd that runes continued to be significantly used. In Scandinavian countries they frequently continued using runic script on gravestones when they had gone over to other methods for everything else, and I sometimes wonder if it was more out of a sense of applying deliberately antiquated language for a sense of history, just as we might label a place "Ye Olde Tea Shoppe."

One has to remember, that in a mainly illiterate society, simple reading and writing would be regarded as magical in itself by those not trained in it, which would probably be a large percentage of the population. The people who were educated ie. leaders and priesthood would derive a certain amount of personal power just by being in on the secret.

Names given to the runes vary considerably in form and spelling. Of the two given for each symbol, the first is more associated with Anglo Saxon language, the second with the Germanic languages.

Symbol	Sound	Names	Associations
ᚠ	f	feoh, fehu	Cattle, wealth, Frey
ᚢ	ur	ur, uruz	Aurochs, strength
ᚦ	th	thorn, thurisaz	Giant, obstacle, attack
ᚨ	a/o	os, as, ansuz	God, mouth
ᚱ	r	rad, raido	Wagon, travel
ᚲ	k	ken, kennaz	Torch, light, knowledge
ᚷ	g	gyfu, gebo	Gift, sex
ᚹ	w/v	wyn, wunjo	Joy, good news
ᚺ	h	hagel, hagalaz	Hail, bad weather, air
ᚾ	n	nid, naudiz	Need, distress
ᛁ	i	isa, isaz	Ice, stasis
ᛃ	j/y	gera, jeraz	Harvest, year, fruitful
ᛇ	eo	eoh, yr, ihwaz	Yew, bow, earth
ᛈ	p	peorth, perthro	Unknown, birth, dicecup
ᛉ	e	elhaz, algiz	Protection, elk
ᛊ	s	sigil, sowilo	Sun, heat
ᛏ	t	tyr, tiwaz	Tyr, courage, battle
ᛒ	b	beorth, berkanan	Birch, healing, woman
ᛖ	eh	ehwho, ehwaz	Horses, adventure
ᛗ	m	man, mannaz	Man, Mankind
ᛚ	l	laguz, laukaz	Leek, water
ᛜ	ing	ing, ingwaz	The God Ing
ᛟ	o	odal, othala	Home, land, tribe
ᛞ	d	Daeg, dagaz	Day, balance

Within the myths, Bragi was given the power to speak with eloquence and poetry by having the runes carved onto his tongue.

On top of that, it is clear that magical attributes were given to each rune. Some of these are evident from the rune poems that have survived from Iceland, Norway and England, where each verse details the properties of an individual rune. For example, feoh the first rune phonetically makes an f sound, but each rune has an idea associated with it as well. In the case of feoh, this is cattle, which were a measure of someone's moveable wealth. Look at the table opposite and you will see the associations for each of the 24 runes in the Elder Futhark.

You can obtain many books on runes, and most will contain extended meanings and associations for each character. They are all valid to the individual authors, but are not all based on hard historical fact. For that reason, I have chosen to not add to the many conflicting ideas by giving you the basic details only. There is another book in this series 'Runes for beginners' by Kristyna Arcati if you wish to study further, plus all of those in the reading list at the end of this chapter.

You can use runes in several ways, and obviously writing is the primary one. Our ancestors were very fond of inscribing their possessions with names etc. Sometimes they wrote out the whole futhark, maybe figuring their magic would cover every eventuality! When you write in runes, it is most usual to write phonetically ie. as words sound, not as they appear in modern English (or any other language as written in Roman letters.) So, for example if you wanted to write the word 'fearing' you would just use feoh, is, rad & ing. You can also use some runes as a sort of shorthand, when they stand for a generally recognised idea e.g. You could simply use the feoh rune instead of writing out the word cattle.

The Roman writer Tacitus describes the Teutonic tribes as marking slivers of fruiting tree wood, and casting them onto a white cloth to make a divination before any important decision was taken. Some of us still do that today. Methods vary, but many depend on a three rune system, in which the first represents the person and their question, the second the possible answer, and the third the eventual consequences leading on from the situation. One can devise all sorts of more complicated systems, none of which will have historic origins but will be effective if you use them consistently, confidently and they mean something to you personally.

This personal relationship with runes is something you can only build up by repeated study and meditation. They are a hard and demanding master or mistress, but rewarding with it. When one has a firm idea of what a rune means personally to you, one can use it in magic. You can chant it, inscribe it on a talisman or make the shape of in the air with a staff, wand or finger. You can even put your own body into runic postures, and more than one person has tried to develop a form of 'runic yoga'.

One way in which runes can be used very powerfully is to combine several together into what is known as a sigil or bindrune. One does have to be very careful when doing this though, as it is very easy to create a third unwanted rune from combining two others together, as I show below.

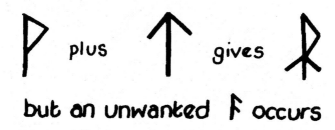

The runic futhark is usually divided into three aetts. The first third is Freyjas Aett, the second Hagels Aett and the last Tyrs Aett. (See below) Historically, the runes always seem to have followed the same order, with the occasional exception of the very last two, odal and daeg, which have sometimes switched places.

Freyjas Aett

Hagels Aett

Tyrs Aett

You might not want others to read and decipher what your intentions are, so bindrunes can be quite useful in this. The other way is to use a code. I have given a couple of examples of codes from history. If you used these, others could read the same sources and decipher them, so you are best to devise your own. Each example uses a two part code. The first number indicated refers to the aett (or family of eight if you prefer to think of it that way) in which the rune occurs. The second number indicates that particular runes order within that aett.

Whisker and Tent runes

Practice

1. Now try coding some runes for yourself. Start by writing gyfu as a `whisker' code. Then write tyr and ken in the form of a `tent rune.'

2. Write your own name in runes. Do not forget to spell it how it sounds, rather than how it is spelt in Roman characters. That means double letters are only written once (such as the double n in my name Jennings) and that some names may appear shorter due to a rune making the sound of several letters e.g. A single thorn rune substitutes for letters `th'

3. Read the figure below. What does it say?

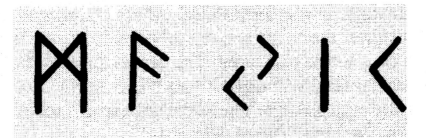

4. Why not make your own set of runes? It is far better both magically and cheaper than buying them. Choose a tree branch about 3cm in diameter of a variety that bears fruit or nuts. If you cannot find a good naturally fallen branch, ask the trees permission (and the owners!) before you cut it, and leave a gift in return. Dry it out naturally, and saw it into slices. You will need at least 24 for the Elder Futhark, including a few spares in case of mistakes in carving. Then carve the shape of a rune onto each, meditating on its meaning and shape as you do so. (You might like to spread this exercise over a long time period.) When they are carved, colour the indentations red. Some people add a few drops of their own blood to the paint to bond them personally to the runes. Finally, varnish them, and make a drawstring bag to keep them safely together. Incidentally, some people make a blank `wyrd' rune as part of a set, to represent the unknown. I have yet to see any convincing historical evidence for the existence of such an idea, and regard the peorth rune as serving this purpose.

5. Try and read several peoples interpretations of the runes. Inevitably, many books draw upon the limited archaeological artefacts available as a source of knowledge. Make sure though you read translations of the old rune poems, which are reproduced in several of the books listed.

Recommended Reading
Kristyna Arcati - *Runes for beginners* (Hodder & Stoughton Headway)
Dr. James M. Peterson - *The Enchanted Alphabet* (Aquarian)
Nigel Pennick - *The Secret Lore of Runes and other Ancient Alphabets* (Rider)
R.I. Page - *Reading the past: Runes* (British Museum)
Jan Fries - *Helrunar,* a manual of rune magick (Mandrake)
Edred Thorsson - *At the Well of the Wyrd: A handbook of Runic Divination* (Weiser) *Runelore* (Weiser)
J.M. Kemble - *Anglo Saxon Runes* (1840 reprint) (Anglo Saxon)
Tony Linsell - *Anglo Saxon Runes* (Book & cards) (Anglo Saxon)
Michael Howard - *Mysteries of the Runes* (Capall Bann)
Osborn & Longland - *Rune Games* (Penguin)
Lisa Peschel - *A Practical Guide to the Runes* (Llewelyn)
Keith Morgan - *Rune Magick* (Pentacle Enterprises)
Bernard King - *The Elements of the Runes* (Element)
Stephen Pollington - *Rudiments of Runelore* (Anglo Saxon)

Chapter 5

Clues from Folklore

Folk customs frequently preserve knowledge that would otherwise be lost, because oral traditions have been marginilised for centuries by academics. They frequently find it hard to accept that a truth can survive (albeit in a sometimes distorted form) without the benefit of someone writing about it. This still happens today, despite the fact that historians do often find elements of truth independently, that are confirmed by the traditions they have previously ignored.

Before we can use folk traditions as a tool for learning about heathen beliefs, we need to have a firm idea of what constitutes a folk tradition. Folklorists like me will argue all night on that one (and frequently do!) so to simplify matters I will give you my personal definition: A song, dance or custom, that has been carried on, mainly by being handed down from one person to another orally, for a long time, say 100 years or more. It should have survived without the major interference of authority (such as school, church) in its performance, which is principally carried on because the people involved want it to.

That might all sound a bit long winded, but it means that people carry things on purely because they want to and that the custom still has some meaning for them. Inevitably, this will mean that the custom may well change over the years to accommodate changing social conditions or attitudes. It also means that folk customs should not become fossilised museum pieces - they must remain alive and adaptable to mean something to the participants. When they fail to have meaning, the custom will be dropped, or carry on only as a confused, archaic parody of itself.

Carrying on those traditions is an important responsibility, and in Viking society, a *skald* ie. a poet who wrote, disclaimed and sang about the historic events of his community, was regarded with awe as the living history book of the tribal group. A leader is not great unless someone says so, and maybe that's why skalds were held in very high regard. It is evident also that the tribal leaders themselves were expected to have a grasp of poetry, as well as being able to fight and speak the law.

Of course, we have nearly lost many traditions through changes in society. Cromwell's Puritans suppressed a large number of customs in the 1600s; the police have called a halt to many more over the years that were perceived as too drunken and rowdy. The invention of the record player and radio stifled many a traditional singer, ashamed at what were now thought of as old fashioned country yokel songs. Yet whenever the end seems nigh, the strength of some of the songs, dances and customs succeeds in winning a new generation of enthusiasts. We also continue to invent and discard many new customs. In recent years I have seen the spread of laying flowers at the spot where a person has died, rather than at the cemetery, and the imported custom of extravagant street carnival has established itself firmly in Notting Hill, London as an exuberant event that is larger than the one in Rio.

Most English speaking people are very unaware of the rich variety and depth of our folklore. There are thousands of traditional songs, dances, stories and customs, very often happening under the noses of people who do not appreciate what we possess. Not every bit of folklore contains Pagan belief, and the ill informed and badly researched writers who have labelled everything as Pagan fertility customs have a lot to answer for. In his valuable book *"The Stations of the Sun"*, Prof. Ronald Hutton explodes some of those myths by showing that many traditions did not start until mediaeval times, hardly a heyday of rampant Paganism. He also (quite accurately in my opinion) attacks the theories presented by Frazer's monumental collection of traditions from around the world `Golden Bough`, which has falsely held sway with academics for the best part of this century. The details of the many native religious practices he researched are good, but suggesting that they all have a connection back to one particular belief and priesthood is patently absurd. However, *Golden Bough* remains a valuable source of raw data if one takes its conclusions with a large sprinkling of the stuff that lives in the saltpot.

Do not let these arguments put you off exploring our rich folk heritage, but be aware of the pitfalls. Prof. Hutton's apparent distrust of anything that hasn't got a written record can be as restricting to the truth as believing everything you are told. Remember that most customs today are ignored by those who write, let alone a few centuries ago, when the upper classes often kept a greater distance from the quaint practices of the peasantry. In my own experience, I have enquired at tourist board offices, town halls, newspapers and libraries about customs currently happening on their own doorstep, to be confronted by complete ignorance. I have gone into churches and pointed out green man carvings that do not appear either in the official church guide or the mind of the vicar.

There is an exciting world out there waiting to be explored by the enthusiastic and open minded Pagan. Not all of the folklore I am about to detail is strictly of the Norse or Anglo Saxon traditions, but it is native to this land and in most cases it is impossible to be certain of the origins of traditions because they are so old. By looking and listening, we can get a feel for the beliefs of our ancestors. There is no substitute for actually experiencing a folk event, be it finding a Pagan carving, watching morris dancers or listening to a traditional singer. Looking at photographs and listening to recorded music does not convey the same sense of occasion and atmosphere. All the time you are experiencing these things, try to think what is going on beneath the surface of jollity and drinking.What is the meaning of that bizarre man/woman sweeping the way clear for the dancers? Would a magical view clarify the storyline of the song being sung? Could the movements of the dance be used as a way of raising energy in a ritual? Would the music, exhaustion, dizziness and working in unity with other people provide a way of reaching an altered state of consciousness?

Sacred Sites

Most stone circles and monoliths have their origins in prehistory, but a large percentage has continued to be used for Pagan rituals throughout the centuries. In many old churches, carvings that have little to do with Christianity and far more to do with natural deities can be found. They can be inside or outside, obvious or obscure. Look out for the green man, with foliage issuing from his mouth, or the woodwose with striped bare skin and a club. In some areas the sheila-na-gig can be found, a female figure displaying her vulva, whilst elsewhere tongue pokers of either sex can be found in stone carvings, wooden bench ends or as gargoyles. I have a liking for dragons and other mythical beasts, but these are often shown being defeated by saints. You can sometimes find the figure of a man with a lion, calf, and eagle. These are the symbols of Matthew, Mark, Luke & John of the Christian gospels, showing how they once borrowed heavily from the earlier Heathen imagery that they tried to supplant.

The Green Man

Dance & Ritual Drama

Best known of English traditions is the morris dance. Whether it had Pagan origins or not is hard to say, but it certainly feels that way now. There are several different variants: The Cotswold Tradition is the best known, as a collection of dances from villages in the Oxfordshire area. It is danced in white clothes, with bells on the legs and handkerchiefs or sticks being used by sides of six men. Some morris men claim it is a males only dance, but there is historical evidence to the contrary, such as the woman who accompanied Will Kemp on a marathon dance in the mid 1600s. Today you can see men's, ladies and mixed sides. The dancers of the North West Tradition (from that part of England) wear clogs, and process along in their dances, rather than staying in one spot. The Border Morris of the Welsh Borders also wears clogs, but also black their faces. In East Anglia and Kent the Molly Dance has been revived, in which the dancers wear farm labourer's clothes or suits of tatters, and often black their faces in ritual disguise. Most areas have sides that dance traditions other than their own as well. Some morris sides are associated with other folk spectacles, such as providing mummers plays, which are traditional, ritualised death - and - resurrection plays with magic and laughter in them. Ritual sword dancers also frequently re-enact ritual murder as they lock swords around their captains throat in mock decapitation. Of course, you do not have to belong to a dance side to experience English folk dance. In recent years there has been a huge revival in

Abbots Bromley Horn Dance

interest in barn dances, or *ceilidhs* as they are sometimes known. The usual pattern is for everyone to be walked through the dance first, so even complete beginners can have a great nights fun, to the sound of traditional folk music.

There are other specific events that happen at different times of the year. The 'Oss at Padstow, the Abbotts Bromley Horn Dance, the Burning Barrels at Ottery St. Mary and the Haxey Hood Game are just a few of the many annual seasonal festivals. In most parts of England there are old customs relating to beating the bounds of a parish, administering a charity or quit rent, conducting a mock trial or election etc. Some have continuous histories going back many hundreds of years, whilst some have been rediscovered and revived. You can locate many of them from the recommended reading.

I am proud to take part in two events in my native East Anglia myself, and would urge all Heathens to support or join in whatever is appropriate in your own area. Each year, my Hearth makes a Jack of the Green figure for me to wear, of branches of greenery, which we bring to life in a ritual on the eve of Mayday. On Mayday morning, we get up to greet the sunrise over the sea at Felixstowe (at around 5.15am) with the East Suffolk Morris Men, and I wear the suit of leaves, which completely covers me. They always like to have the Jack of the Green present when they dance up the Mayday sun, just like many of the other dance sides who make the effort that morning.

On December 26th I can be found at Middleton, Suffolk, as part of a Cutty Wren ceremony. Years ago I had read that it was the only place in England that had such a tradition, but it had died out around the turn of the century. Chatting to some dancers and musicians in a pub session one night, the idea was born to revive the event. A molly dance team Old Glory was formed, and we have a torchlit procession, led with a carved wooden wren, dancing and music. Each year I sing the traditional songs and retell the story of how the wren became the king of the birds. There must be many such customs waiting for the right people to revive them. It certainly means something to the people taking part or watching, as over 100 turn out each year for it, despite it being part of the Xmas holiday. You will notice that in reviving it we have used a carved wren, not a killed one. This is just one of the ways in which traditions adapt to changes in public attitude.

Folksong & Music

Very few British folksongs are explicit about magic and the supernatural, but it is sometimes possible to gain a magical understanding of them from some small clue. There were times when it was dangerous to sing about such things anyway. One must also remember that the bulk of our repertoire today was saved for us by collectors going round at the turn of the century, who feared many would die out with industrialisation and mass entertainment. Many of those collectors were Christian vicars, whose informants were often shy about revealing some of their bawdier material to such men. One must remember this was the Victorian age, with a hypocritical and prudish attitude to anything regarded as un - Christian, and if a collector did manage to take down a risqué ballad, he could never publish it as such.

If you hear a line in a song referring to `A Gay Green Gown' it often refers to a witch or magician. There is one song called just that from the New Forest, together with some others contained in an out of print book by Ruth Tongue called `The Chime Child.' In `The Broomfield Wager', recorded by several people including the man who I learnt it from, Cyril Poacher, the broom is an ingredient to a magic sleeping draught. The woman outwits the man in it, returning from a field with her virginity intact, despite his assistant's magic actions.

58

Without that explanation, the song makes little sense. There is a similar but more obvious theme of male magician trying to bed a female magician in `The Two Magicians', recorded by amongst others, Steeleye Span. They have made some splendid recordings of many other magical songs as well, including `Thomas the Rhymer' and `Tam Lin', which are both songs about people seized by the fairy folk. Also in their repertoire are versions of three ritualistic murder songs, `Little Sir Hugh', `Outlandish Knight' and `Long Lankin'. Other songs to watch out for are the various Cutty Wren songs, seasonal songs for maying etc, John Barleycorn, and two about mythical beasts exaggerated to monstrous proportions, `Derby Ram' and `Lambton Worm'. If you ever come across a Scottish song called `Nicky Tans' (about the string you tie around the bottom of trouser legs) it has a single line in it referring to "the horseman's grip and word", the only time I have detected a mention of horse whisperers magic.

Practice

1. Go out and see if you can find some interesting carvings of the types I have mentioned.

2. Try to visit an ancient sacred site, such as a stone circle or standing stone. Take your time, and be quiet and respectful around it. Place your hands on the rock and see if you can feel a vibration from it. Take a compass, and check how the site is aligned. Does the compass behave erratically when near the stones? They sometimes do.

3. Go and see some traditional singing, dancing or custom, and join in if possible. Can you use anything you experienced within a ritual setting?

4. Research the folklore of the area in which you live. Is there any event worth reviving or one in decay that could do with a fresh injection of life? The English Folk Dance and Song Society (EFDSS) have a research library, the address of which is shown below.

Recommended Reading
Sir James Frazer - *The Golden Bough* (Papermac)
Prof. Ronald Hutton - *The Stations of the Sun* (Oxford)
Brian Shuel - *National Trust Guide to Traditional Customs of Britain* (National Trust)
Williams & Lloyd - *Penguin Book of English Folk Songs* (Penguin)
Roy Palmer - *Everymans Book of English Country Songs* (Dent)
Marion Green - *A Harvest of Festivals* (Longman)
Frances Child - *The English & Scottish Popular Ballads* (Houghton Mifflin) *Oxford Book of Ballads* (Oxford)
Christina Hole - *A Dictionary of Folk Customs* (Paladin)
Michael Howard - *The Sacred Ring* (Capall Bann)
Nigel Pennick - *Crossing the Borderlines: Guising, Masking and Ritual animal Disguises in the European Tradition* (Capall Bann)
The Green Man - Anderson & Hicks (Harper Collins)
 English Dance and Song magazine and The Folk Directory - available from the English Folk Dance and Song Society, Cecil Sharp House, 2, Regents Park Rd, London, NW1 7AY

Recommended Listening
There is no substitute for seeing and hearing folk traditions in live performance, but if that is impossible listen to:
Various - *English Customs & Traditions* (Saydisc CD-SDL 425) Includes Padstow, Helston, Castleton, Abbots Bromley, Mummers etc.
The Watersons - *Frost and Fire* (Topic)Ritual songs

Steeleye Span - Best of (Chrysalis CDP 321487-2) Includes Little Sir Hugh, Long Lankin, Demon Lover, Elf Call, Thomas the Rhymer.

Steeleye Span - *Time* (Park PRKCD34) Includes Cutty Wren, The Elf Knight plus two contemporary Pagan songs

Fairport Convention - *Liege and Lief* (Chrysalis CDP 3214672) Includes Tam Lin

Chapter 6

Living With the Norse Tradition Today

The Norse Tradition is not a glorified re-enactment society, of people dressing up in costume and imitating their ancestors. It promotes the spirit of their age, rather than the actuality. In any case, the much vaunted rape, pillage and plunder would be rather frowned upon nowadays! The Vikings were very modern, forward looking people for their time, using the best of available technology. They also had a specific mythology and religion we can still relate to, even if we cannot emulate the way they carried it out. For example, like most religions at that time they did sacrifice humans, certainly at the temple at Uppsala, Sweden, and probably at the grave mounds of important people (as the Anglo Saxons did at the Sutton Hoo, England burials.)

Unless you are willing to study Old Norse or Old English you are not going to be able to conduct rituals in that same language. Some people do just that, and provide a translation for others, but of course although they can write rituals in the language, very few words of ritual have survived from those times. So, as modern Odinists we are faced with the task of reconstructing rituals, or developing new ones, using whatever clues have been left in written texts, pictures and folklore. We can use details we know from the mythology (e.g. the hammer used in blessing a wedding), as a focus for the modern words and actions we put together.

It is no good though constructing rituals for gatherings, unless they are allowed to have a practical effect on one's daily life. One can live the faith in many ways, dependent on your capabilities and situation. I actually changed career as a result of my Heathen beliefs from sales to counselling, which I saw as being more related to my spiritual path. One may choose to mix with a particular circle of friends who are sympathetic to one's beliefs, or to get involved in helping the survival of our threatened environment. Some of the ways in which you react on a daily basis may be dictated by the particular path one chooses within the tradition. Someone aspiring to be a *gothi* (priest or priestess) must have regular contact with other people, whilst a more shamanic role such as *volva* would demand that its practitioner spend a lot of time close to nature, in the countryside.

There is also a sense of how one faces adversity as an individual within the Norse Tradition. The examples from the past show us that an Odinist would stay true to their word and tribe, whatever the personal cost, often with a stoic or fatalistic view of life based on the concept of the web of the *wyrd*. A promise is seen as a sacred thing, so one does not give them lightly.

A mead horn

Generosity is a much vaunted attribute in many Saxon and Norse texts, especially 'ring giving', in which a faithful warrior or servant is rewarded with arm or finger rings, a form of currency. He can choose to pass part of that honour on to his wife or children who may have assisted him in some way. Thus, honour is publicly spread, and the bond between the giver and receiver strengthened.

One must also live as closely as possible to the Havamal, and as that is largely concerned with hospitality, one must seek to be both a generous and welcoming host and a valued guest. It is the custom in many of our families for the lady of the house to offer mead to visitors on arrival. (Mead bearers are traditionally women, but of course in this day and age, there is no reason why the honour cannot be shared.) On a practical note, have you considered brewing your own mead, wine or beer? There is a great emphasis on practical skills within our tradition, and this one combines the satisfaction of being independent and thrifty with enjoyment and personally providing a part of the feast that accompanies each ritual or guest welcoming.

We must study our chosen path well, and not be afraid to defend it against all comers. Our directness can be seen as confrontational to others (including the wider Pagan community at times) but is a result of trying to live open, honest lives, respecting the role of women and nature, and striving to maintain a good reputation.

That can sometimes place one in an ethical dilemma. For example, imagine confronting a burglar in your house in the middle of the night. He has ripped the phone from the wall and is threatening you and your family. Some Pagan paths would dictate that "And it harm none" still applies and one should allow him to leave with the stolen property, only using violence if he attacks first. The idea of karmic retribution comes into it somewhere. My position, and that of many others of our tradition would be to attack, as hard as possible with whatever came to hand. I would not leave it for him to make the first move, as whoever gets in first usually wins in these situations. It is not anything to do with bravery - I have a right and a duty to protect my home and family. Of course, English law would take a very different view, and whilst a court may be sympathetic, they could not condone an attack that went beyond self defence. The ethical catch is, that Odinists are supposed to uphold the law. In fact, in ancient Iceland, each gothi priest was also a law speaker. ie. The two activities were intertwined. It makes for some hard choices as to how one works out ones personal standards and where to draw the line. No one else can tell you what to do. As a member of the Norse Tradition one should be independent and free thinking, capable of deciding your own answers.

Practice

1. What would you do in the situation with the burglar, and why?

2. Find an environmental activity that you can get involved in. It could be recycling your household waste, nature conservation work or forming part of a protest action against something that threatens the natural environment.

3. How open can you be about your beliefs? Some people will have natural difficulties in `coming out' to their family, friends or workplace. Consider how you can best deal with this, in a way that informs without trying to proselytise. Also, is it wiser to leave some people in ignorance, or will it cause continuing tension as they make false assumptions about your beliefs?

4. How about having a go at some home brewing. There are plenty of books available on how to make wine and beer, but I have included one in the list below that will enable you to make the ritual honey drink of Norse mythology, mead.

Recommended Reading

Lee M. Hollander - *The Saga of the Jomsvikings* (University of Texas)
Nigel Pennick - *Practical Magic in the Northern Tradition* (Thoth)
Stephen Flowers (who also writes as Edred Thorsson) - *The Galdabrok: An Icelandic Grimoire* (Weiser) *Fire and Ice* (Llewellyn)
Gothrun Dimmbla - *Odsmal* (Freyjukkettir)
Alby Stone - *The Well of Ymir* (Heart of Albion Press)
Freyja Aswynn - *Northern Mysteries & Magic* (Llewellyn) (Previously published as *The Leaves of Yggdrassil*)
Francis Beswick - *Traditional British Honey Drinks* (Heart of Albion Press)
Pagan Dawn magazine (The Pagan Federation, BM Box 7097, London, WC1N 3XX)

Chapter 7

It's Magic!

In the *Saga of King Hrolf* we get a few glimpses of some powerful magic at work. Queen Skuld chants incantations to defeat opposing warriors, and from the magic she weaves from a scaffold erected in a black tent, a monstrous boar appears, shooting arrows from it's bristles. One wonders if this is the magic of *fylga* ie. Projecting ones spirit into a remote situation as a 'fetch'. Certainly some sectors of the Asatru tradition believe in a guardian spirit called a *hamingja,* which can attack or be attacked.

A more gentle kind of magic is at work in the *Saga of Eirik the Red,* when a visiting volva called Thorbjorg, the Little Sibyl is welcomed at Brattahlid, Iceland. She arrived wearing a blue cloak with jewelled straps right down to the hem, a black lambskin hood lined with white catskin, glass beads about her neck and a staff topped with a brass knob and set with stones. She wore a touchwood belt from which hung a skin bag for her charms. Hairy calfskin shoes and catskin gloves completed the outfit. She was honoured with the best of food, and given a high seat, with hen feather cushion, to survey the assembled throng. She asked for assistance from the women in chanting a spell called Varthlokur, or Spiritlocks, but only one, a Christianised woman called Gudrid was able to, after some reluctance. The text goes on to say all the women gathered in a circle around the platform on which Thorbjorg was seated and the chant was eventually recited by Gudrid, after which prophecy was given. Both these examples would seem to fit into what we would term seidr, that intuitive, and largely feminine based magic of the Norse Tradition.

Note that there is both the positive and negative at work here. The sagas do not contain any equivalent of the wiccan 'An it harm none' ethic. That is not to say that one should not be applied now, as an ethical way of working. I am a firm believer that there is a cost for all magic performed, good or bad, and that evil will bring its own reward. Although there may not be specific texts telling you not to work magic for negative ends, there are plenty that will tell you that your good reputation and the way you face adversity are very important.

Such considerations obviously never bothered the mother Helga and Aunt Frakokk of Harold Hakonarson (Smooth Tongue), Earl of Orkney, in the *Orkneyinga saga*. They prepared a white linen shirt, threaded with gold, for his brother Paul. When Harold put it on instead, his flesh started to quiver, and he died in agony, in place of his brother. In that same saga, the mother of Sigurd helps her son overcome being outnumbered seven to one in battle by means of a magical raven banner she weaves. It has the property of ensuring victory, but at the cost of each of its bearers being killed in the battles.

Men work their magic too in the sagas, but in different ways, often by use of the runes. In *Egils saga* the hero corrects the badly written runes of another that are causing a sick girl to get worse rather than better, and one can take that as a lesson to us all in being careful in our choice and inscription of runes. In the *Saga of the Jomsvikings* both King Gorm and Earl Harold pay great attention to their dreams and visions. There are stories to of warriors doing battle with supernatural fiends, such as the battle between Grettir and Glam, in the *Saga of Grettir the Strong*. Elsewhere we find that the priests of Freyja sensed when she was present within a decorated wagon. This was paraded around the district, and no disputes could continue at this time. Finally, it was taken to a lake to be washed, and the slaves who had performed this service executed afterwards. This is all a highly ceremonial form of magic, known as *galdr*, although it also relies on intuition as well.

Galdr magic can be quite imitative in the way it works. e.g. Writing an illness down on a piece of paper and then destroying it, with the intention of getting rid of the illness to. Taking that to a more elaborate level, there was a way of cursing someone known as the niding pole (from Old Norse *nidhstong*). A pole with a curse or ritual insult is left outside the victim's door in secret, during the night. Sometimes it is topped with the head or skull of an animal, such as a horse. I would surmise that anyone finding such an item confronting them in the morning would be disturbed, whether they

The Oseburg wagon, Norway

believed in magic or not! So something disturbing passes a feeling on to its victim. There is a tale of a bad king being driven out of his land by a powerful magician setting up a niding pole on the shore, facing landwards. It was considered bad luck to moor the Viking dragonships with their fearsome dragons figureheads facing a friends land, as they would scare or insult the *landvattir* (land spirits). Some at least had detachable figureheads. I suppose on a practical note, having your ship facing down the beach for a quick getaway often made sense as well!

A primary source of magic has to be the runes though, and the carving of runes (by one sometimes termed a vitki) is sometimes referred to as *Taufr* ie. Talismatic magic. One can see the enigmatic reference to the runic "nine lays of power" detailed in the Havamal, which has verses about runes

A valknut

dulling the blades of enemies and deflecting their arrows or magic to loosing the shackles of a prisoner, gaining a woman or calming an angry sea. I guess not all that would be of much practical use today, but it begets the important question, what is magic?

From the myths we can see that some types of magic are not common to all Gods and Goddesses. Loki borrows Freyjas falcon feather cloak to fly, and Thor is not ashamed to ask the witch Groa to try remove the whetstone fragment from his head. Someone once defined magic as bending natural forces to ones will. I would add that as we are part of a nature religion, if we are in tune with the natural world, then we must be part of it, and be part of it's inherent forces, bending with them. There is nothing more magic for me than seeing a delicate plant forcing its way up through a crack in the concrete to flower. It knows it's will and is doing it. One of the prime aspects of many forms of magic is to really know one's own will (for which you really need to know yourself) and then to project it. That is not a *carte blanche* to do what ever you want, since a person in tune with themself is rarely destructive, coercive or malignant. Some people define magic in two parts, higher and lower, where the higher part corresponds to knowing and changing ones self, and the lower to mundane workings such as healing others or improving situations.

How you work magic will be up to you and your personal background and preferences. Whatever you do, think it through first. It is better to do nothing than do the wrong thing, and whenever you use magic you are interfering, even if it is with the best of intentions. Each spell you cast will have consequences, both immediate and as a knock on effect. (Think back to the imagery of the Web of the Wyrd, where one tug on a thread causes the whole to vibrate.) You must consider whether what you are doing is truly useful in the long term, or will only be a short term gain. Let me give you a couple of examples;

Consider someone who has injured their wrist. The obvious practical thing to do is to get them to seek conventional medical advice and treatment. Magic should be a last resort, not a first response. Anyway, having had it bandaged up, they come to you for relief of some of the pain. You could do a healing spell over it, maybe for example chanting/ writing *laguz* or *beorth,* two runes associated with healing. But stop and think first! If the pain is relieved, will the person then use the hand, instead of resting it, causing longer term problems. After all, pain is often nature's way of getting us to stop doing harmful things to ourselves. Also, what if you think of the injury of being there for a purpose? It might prevent that person from playing tennis tomorrow, and thus not being introduced to the man who will swindle them out of their savings. See what I mean by knock on effects? That is not to say you should not do healing spells, but you might for a start check what the recipient is going to do if they feel better, and put the onus on them to ask you for a spell, rather than you take responsibility for laying it on them.

Lets look at another popular area of magic that connected with romance. Suppose a young lady came to you asking for a bit of magical help in getting together with that dishy, unattached guy she sees at the bus stop. Ok, lets imagine you make a powerful ritual to bring them together. It works, and they get married. A few months into the marriage, the lady discovers she is married to a wife beater. Now, was it black or white magic you worked? Certainly the intention was good, but the trouble with wishes and magic is that you do not always quite know what you are asking for. Was it fair also to work against the mans natural actions ie. not chatting her up before, thus taking away his choice in the matter? I think that the popular images of black and white magic are misleading - most of it is in various hues of grey. If you worried about every consequence, you would not work magic at all, which some would say was preferable. However, with such an exciting and powerful tool at our disposal it is hard to resist the temptation to use it, and I think the main safeguard must be to examine your motivations closely beforehand.

Of course, that is not the only precaution you must take whilst doing magic. Just as a professional electrician always protects himself from the power, and creates a safe working space, so must you.This is usually achieved by creating a sacred space in which to work. Only people and objects which you trust are allowed there, and protection is asked for from the deities and natural elements and spirits. Usually, the space is a circle, but there is no reason why it cannot be another shape. The Ve sacred enclosures of the Norse and Saxon peoples are believed to have possibly been square. They had a rule about not coming armed into it, although I believe they must have allowed at least one knife for sacrificing and carving an animal, which they frequently did as part of their rituals. These were known as blots, possibly in connection with the word blood, which was sprinkled all around the area and on the participants.

Sometimes individuals built temples, such as Hrafnkel, the priest of Frey, who according to the Icelandic saga made many sacrifices, giving half his treasures to Frey. There were priestesses too, who were probably more associated with Freys sister Freyja. Some of these certainly worked in partnership, such as Thorthur Freysgothi (Freys priest) and his sister who was known as Thurithur Hofgytha (temple priestess) of Freysnes, Iceland, who are referred to in Landnamabok, the Book of Settlements. You will notice that they are given the titles *gothi* and *gytha* (priest and priestess) which we most associate with more formal galdr magic, but the Goddesss Freyja who they serve is said to be the bringer of the more shamanic Seidr magic. This demonstrates how then, like today, there are no clear boundary lines over roles and which magic they use.

Ritual magic can take many different forms, and it is up to you how you perform it. There is no right or wrong way, only what feels appropriate for you. Some people like to plan rituals in advance, and try to always do certain actions the same way. I always try and teach my pupils to make very definite physical ritual actions to complement their very definite thoughts. If you are presenting a Thorshammer to hallow something, hold it firm, and make clear movements. You are not waving a banana about! If you look at Anglo Saxon verse charms they do not ask for something to be done. They are that positive they say it has been done, already. The magician is confident that the stolen property is being returned, or the cows are giving more milk even as they speak!

Ritual dancing figure detail from the Sutton Hoo helmet

Others prefer to rely upon the inspiration of the moment, rather than the pre-planned ritual, although this is more prone to mistakes. You might like to do quiet meditative pathworkings, runic carving and speak whispered words, or you might want to dance, (like the figure on the Sutton Hoo helmet illustration) chant runes at the top of your voice and beat drums loud enough to wake the dead. If your choice falls towards the latter be warned - however far you get away from civilisation, sound carries through a wood at night, and you might find yourself summoning the police to your circle instead of the hoped for deity! Actually, I never summon anything myself - I believe one should have the good manners to ask politely. It is a matter of what attitude one has towards the deities. Our tradition does not teach a craven attitude though, as the myths show gods and goddesses who appreciate fierce independence rather than cowering timidity, so I guess kneeling and sycophancy are out as far as our religion are concerned.

Practice

1. Why not try creating a simple spell? There are plenty of books willing to give you step by step instructions, but the Norse Tradition teaches independence and individual self sufficiency, so try inventing your own. It will be just as valid as anything you can read elsewhere, but will have the additional potency of being personalised and understood by you as an individual. Just to get you started, here are a few elements you might like to incorporate; Burning candles and incense, marking out your sacred space with a staff, wand, sword or whatever. Chanting or writing runes. Making up a poem or song to sing. Setting up a rhythm with claps, stamps, rattles or drums. Preparing some food or drink to be consumed as

part of the magic. I am sure you can think of many more original elements of your own. This will be very good preparation for the next chapters work on rituals.

Recommended Reading
Louis J. Rodrigues - *Anglo Saxon Verse Charms, Maxims & Heroic Legends* (Anglo Saxon)
Michael Harner - *The Way of the Shaman* (Harper & Row)
Edred Thorrson - *Futhark: A handbook of rune magic* (Weiser) *A Book of Troth, The 9 Doors of Midgard, Rune Might, Northern Magic* (All by LLewellyn)
Kveldulf Gundarsson - *Teutonic Magic* (Llwellyn)
Stephen A McNallen - *Rituals of Asatru* Vol. 1-3 (World Tree)
Jan Fries - *Seidways* (Mandrake)
Sheena McGrath - *Asyniur: Womens Mysteries in the Northern Tradition* (Capall Bann)

Chapter 8

Some Simple Rituals

In Chapter 11 I shall give you some points of contact to network with other members of the Norse Tradition. If there is an Odinist hearth group near where you live, you may be able to join in some of their activities, and get a feeling for what works for you personally. Do not join a group you are unhappy with though. It is better to take a solo path than be pushed along a route you feel uncomfortable with. Do not dabble in magic.You wouldn't dabble in brain surgery and this is far more important. Prepare properly and safeguard yourself. Sooner or later you will have to work by yourself (or with a partner) anyway, whether you are part of a hearth or not.

I would like to give you a starting point to build your rituals from. It will be one of several you can find, including some in the recommended reading. The rituals I will suggest are not definitive. They are there for you to add to, edit or whatever until you reach your own personal plan. Lets start with a sequence that you will need in one form or another for every ritual. As we are a nature religion I assume all rituals are held outdoors unless it is impractical to do so:

Opening and closing a sacred space
Locate North, (with a compass if necessary) and set up your altar space there. A tree stump, box or cloth on the ground will do. Be still and quiet, and concentrate on being in tune with your surroundings. When ready, take a staff or other tool, and trace the outline of a circular (or rectangular,

triangular etc.) working area with it on the ground, big enough for all you wish to do, and to contain all present. I personally start in the East and work clockwise like the sun, but you may have another preference. Next, purify the circle with either some water or blood, sprinkled from a bowl with a branch. You could say something like "I create this sacred space, and purify it, so that all that happens within it will be honourable and good." If you are working with other people, involve them to, sharing out the various duties.

You might like to light candles or incense at some point. If you are working at night, set candles in jars or lanterns, hung on poles driven in the ground. That way you do not have to crawl around the ground to read the words. (Of course, it is better if you can learn the words off by heart, or to be confident in improvising them on the spot so that scripts are not required.)

Illustration of Thorshammer pendants

Next, make an invocation to each of the cardinal points. This can be the sign of Thors hammer, (an inverted T) drawn in the air, together with appropriate invitations to the deities and/or elemental forces you associate with each quarter. Alternatively you may hold a ceremonial hammer in the air. Throughout the world, many cultures associate the same elements with specific directions: East-Air, South-Fire, West-Water, North-Earth. e.g. Your invocations could be:

East: *"Guardians of Austri. Welcome Odin & Frigga, and the spirit of Hraevelgr, whose wings direct the winds."*

South: *"Guardians of Sudri. Welcome Thor and Sif, Balder and Nanna, and the spirit of Surts fire."*

West: *"Guardians of Westri. Welcome Heimdall, and the spirit of Aegirs watery sea."*

North: *"Guardians of Nordri. Welcome Frey & Freyja and the spirit of Fjorgyn & Erce of the earth."*

(The Guardian names are taken from the elemental elves given in the mythology.)

Finally, from the **centre** you could make a general greeting. "I welcome all here, be they Gods, spirits or humans. Let none take offence as we try concentrate our good wishes into the centre of this sacred space. May all that attend here guard and protect the sanctity of this place, and not leave it until the rituals end. May this be a gateway to the nine worlds of Yggdrassil, and our work be as fruitful as Frigga. Let no one disturb a place hallowed with Thor the Thunderer's protection." (All make hammer sign.)

You can now get on with whatever specific ritual you are working that night, be it a baby naming, initiation, handfast wedding or funeral. (I'd advise against all four at the same event!) At some point you should have some food and drink. This is usually towards the end, and can consist of mead, beer, juice or wine and bread, cakes meat or fruit. It is traditional within all parts of the Northern Tradition to do this, and very often the drink is shared from a drinking horn. You should bless the food and drink before distribution, and save a portion to be left as an offering back to the earth that provided it. Suitable blessings might be " We thank Sif for the fruit of her golden hair. May none of us be hungry in the company of another." & "We thank Kvasir for his lifeblood preserved in this mead. May none of us ever be thirsty in the company of another." (Sifs hair is a poetic kenning for corn, and the myths tell of mead coming from Kvasirs death.)

At the end of the nights work you must close down the space properly. It will help to close you down as well, so that you are not wide awake and psychically very aware at four in the morning! Sacred spaces left open and abandoned act as beacons for all sorts of dubious characters, and are a menace to others. Most people reverse the process they start with, so you could go back to the cardinal points in reverse order (East, North, West and South) and say: "Thankyou all for your help and aid within the ritual. Until we meet again we bid you *waes hael!*" (Waes Hael is an Anglo Saxon phrase translating as 'Be hale, or healthy'. It is often used by Heathens as a greeting or farewell phrase. The modern word for a type of seasonal song, wassail derives from it.)

So there you have the framework for an opening or closing, which you can simplify, elaborate and customise. It is important to try and stimulate all the senses in a ritual. In that one you can see that there were sights (candles) smells (incense) sounds (words) tastes (food & drink) and touch (the sprinkling of water). I think it is important to involve everyone present as well, rather than have 'expert' doers and passive 'watchers.'

Practice

1. Customise the opening and closing ritual above for your own tastes and use.

2. Construct a ritual to go into the middle of it. It could be for a funeral, handfasting or any other purpose, but try and utilise all senses. It could be a specific anniversary celebration, such as the Yule or Summer Solstice. Maybe you could incorporate a folk song or dance you learnt in conjunction with chapter 5, or even make up a ritual drama, with parts for everyone, from one of the myths you have read. Do not forget that you can use runes as well, to chant, scribe or as body postures. If actions or words are to be repeated, 3 & 9 are the two numbers of major magical significance within the tradition. You might get some additional ideas from some of the recommended books, both in this and the previous chapters. Certainly try and incorporate any details from the myths and sagas you can that are relevant e.g. In the Lay of Thrym when Thor pretends to be a bride, he is offered food and drink, wears a veil and has a hammer placed in his lap. These are all details you can use in putting together a handfast wedding ceremony. If you were planning a funeral rite, the story of Balder's ship burial contains detail about nine maidens (possibly the wave maiden daughters of Aegir) throwing blue scarves into the air, something quite easily incorporated into a modern rite.

Recommended Reading

Ed Fitch - *Rites of Odin* (Llewellyn)
Donald Tyson - *Rune Magic* (Llewellyn)
D.J. Conway - *Norse Magic* (Llewellyn)
Jan Fries - *Visual Magic & Helrunar* (both Mandrake)

Chapter 9

A Seasonal Cycle

As a nature religion, the Norse Tradition draws upon the phenomena of the natural world, and its cycle of birth, life and death for its seasonal festivals. Most of us are used to thinking in terms of four seasons, and it is not too hard to draw parallels with human development; Birth in spring, maturity in summer, old age in autumn and death in winter. Thus, death is a part of the life cycle, and new birth follows it.

Most of the Teutonic derived tribes seem to have divided the year into two, with spring as a part of summer, and autumn as part of winter. This differs from the Celtic Pagan festival cycle, which starts for them at Samhain on October 31st. The Norse year starts at the Yule solstice, around December 21st, which is known as Mothers Night. No one really knows whether this refers to biological mothers, earth mother or Disir goddesses, or even all three, but it is a great time for a feast and fire to dispel the gloomy cold of winter, and observe the sun starting to get slightly stronger again. Having said all that, you will often find those of the Norse tradition joining their friends of other Pagan paths in celebrating some of the dates on the Celtic calendar. Firstly, some were probably common to both tribes, but anyway, we Vikings always appreciate having a good time!

Many people of our tradition use the solstices and full moons as regular, natural markers for their meetings and rituals. Many also have in recent years designated specific days to commemorate particular aspects of our faith. I have shown these in the accompanying table, together with some moon

Norse Tradition calendar

Asatru	Bede	Roman	Date	Festival	Theme
Snowmoon	Yule/Guili	Jan	17	Charming the plough	Labour
Horningmoon	Solmonath (cakes)	Feb	2	Disir	Imbolc
Horningmoon	Solmonath	Feb	14	Vali	Family
Lentingmoon	Hrethmonath (Goddess)	Mar	20	Summer Finding	Ostara
Ostara	Eostre (Goddess)	Apr	23	Sigurd	Homeland
Ostara	Eostre	Apr	30	Walpurg-isnacht	May eve customs
Merrymoon	Thrimilci (3 milkings)	May	22	Ragnar Lodbrok	Viking hero
Merrymoon	Thrimilci	May	30	Vanir	Vanir
Fallowmoon	Litha (Double size month	Jun	8	Lindis-farne Day	1st raid
Fallowmoon	of Moon)	Jun	21	Midsummer	Balder
Fallowmoon	Litha	Jun	24	Aesir	Aesir
Haymoon	Litha	Jul	15	Alfar	Elves
Haymoon	Litha	Jul	22	Sleipnir	Life
Haymoon	Litha	Jul	30	Perchta Mannus	Lughnas-agh
Harvestmoon	Weodmonath	Aug	24	Runes	The mind
Harvestmoon	(Weeds)	Aug	26	Harvest	Harvest
Sheddingmoon	Halegmonath (Offerings)	Sep	9	Herman of Cherusci	Memories
Sheddingmoon	Halegmonath	Sep	23	Winter-Finding	Harvest end
Huntingmoon	Wintirfylith (1st full moon of winter)	Oct	12	Hengest	Settle-ment
Huntingmoon	Wintirfylith	Oct	approx 19–20	Winter Sat & Sun	Winter
Huntingmoon	Wintirfylith	Oct	31	Hallowe'en	Samhain
Fogmoon	Blotmonath	Nov	1	Heimdall	God
Fogmoon	(Sacrifice)	Nov	11	Einherjar	War hero
Fogmoon	Blotmonath	Nov	23	Wayland Smith	Folk hero
Wolfmoon	Yule/Guili	Dec	1	Ullr	God
Wolfmoon	Yule/Guili	Dec	21	Mother's Night	Mid-Winter

month names used by many in place of the Roman derived calendar. Some take this further by making the spelling of days closer to the original divine connections ie. Sun-day, Moon-day, Tiws-day, Wodens-day, Thors-day, Friggas-day, Sataere-day. You will also find some folk deliberately use a different year number, which is 250 years older than the Christian one. So 1998 becomes 2248 RE. the RE standing for Runic Era.

Of course, there may be other dates which are significant for you, which you want to make part of your annual calendar. If you become involved in carrying out one of the traditional folk customs, this will become an important stage of the year to you. Some people celebrate the anniversary of the first meeting of their hearth group, or their handfast wedding. Others make a point of remembering the day they first worked a ritual, or were initiated into a group. The point is to have a regular calendar of festivals that mean something to you personally to celebrate, not someone else's imposed list. It is worth remembering to that our ancestors did not go in for elaborate fixed date calendars. They were far more likely to judge spring had arrived by the buds sprouting on a particular plant, rather than because it was a certain date. In the accompanying table I have shown some modern month names given by Odinists against both their Romanised equivalents, and the Anglo Saxon names written down by Bede, together with what he thought they signified. I have also indicated some days celebrated by some, but not all of the Norse Tradition.

One can make some specific connections with the mythology and the seasons. For example, the second half of Freygerdas name means frozen field. So in the story of *Skirnirs Journey,* where Frey the fertility God falls in love and seeks to woo her, one might interpret their union as Spring. At the other end of Summer, when Loki cuts Sifs beautiful hair, and has to replace it with spun gold, it is usually assumed to signify the cutting of the golden corn of harvest. Similarly, when the God of goodness and light Balder is sent to Hel, it can be interpreted as the dying of the sun in winter, although one can view it in other ways. The sun and moon have a special place in the Norse creation myths, as they do in most cultures, but does the reference to the ravening wolves Skoll and Hati, chasing them to gobble them up refer to eclipses? I am sure as you read the mythology, you can find many more apparent connections with the natural world.

Sif's corn hair cut by scythe

Practice

1. What dates are significant to you? Why not make up your own personal religious calendar? You may want to refer to some of the books at the end of Chapter 5.

2. Can you find a myth that appears to say something about the natural world?

Recommended Reading
Bob Trubshaw - *Grimrs Year* (Heart of Albion)

Chapter 10

The Hard Questions

The Norse Tradition has so much to offer as a spiritual path, but it obviously has its detractors, both within and outside the world of Paganism. One of its most obvious problems is the association of Nazis with both runes and parts of the mythology. This is a problem faced by most religions. Anything that is a powerful stirrer of emotions will be misused by others to further their own cause. If however, we ban the use of runes on the basis that Nazis used the double sigil as a symbol for the S.S. etc., then we allow them to have won.

I believe it is more appropriate to seize back and reclaim such symbols for their rightful use. After all, Christians did not stop using the crucifix after its adoption by the Klu Klux Klan. The Nazis pushed an ideology of a pure Aryan master race. If you have examined the historical evidence connected with Chapter 2, you will find that the English people are a mixture of Saxon, Jute, Frisian, Dane, Swedish, Jewish, Flemish, Norman etc., and the idea of a pure race becomes laughable. However, that does not stop some racist, homophobic thugs from trying to still use those discredited theories to bolster their own paranoid inadequacies. Unfortunately, some of them have joined or even help run certain Odinist organisations, and do a great discredit to our movement. It is ironic that the Nazis closed down most esoteric organisations and Hitler paid his Catholic Church tax until the day he died! In chapter 11 I will give you the addresses of a couple of UK organisations I believe to be free of such evil influences.

Illustration - Franks casket warriors

The other uninformed criticism levelled at the Norse Tradition is that it cannot be right, coming from such a bloodthirsty lot of raping, pillaging Vikings. I would argue that most of the world's religions have found their roots in ancient, violent civilizations. One could also argue that they continue to flourish in a modern, more violent world, despite their teachings! The Vikings were no better or worse than any of their contemporaries, but were the subject of influential writing by the churchmen they attacked. Much of their beautiful artistry is wrongly attributed today as Celtic (who are not the only race to design complicated knotwork jewellery), and their achievements in exploration, poetry, democratic government, and women's rights are conveniently ignored.

Of course, we have to adapt the ancient beliefs for our modern life, just as other religions who have learnt by experience, such as Christians dispensing with the Inquisition. Human or animal sacrifice is no longer necessary, and it is a bit impractical to have a ship burial today. We can though carry on those historic positive qualities of respect for the natural world, loyalty to ones tribe and living an honourable life. As we have seen in Chapter 7, magic in itself is neutral. It is how we use it that makes it good or bad, black or white. If one lives an honourable life, one would not normally consider using the black magic that one might be capable of, because it would lessen your reputation. I guess that might be the ethical root of why people of our tradition do not use black magic, rather than the more karmic ideal of the wiccan 'An it harm none.'

That leads me on to another question sometimes asked, are we witches? Certainly by the more modern definitions favoured by initiatory movements, such as Gardnerian or Alexandrian Wicca, we are not. We do not have a formalised degree system or chain of initiation. However, the older definition of a witch is simply that of a person who does magic, within the framework of their Pagan beliefs. So every witch is a Pagan, but Pagans who do not try to use magic are not witches in my book. If you attempt magic within our path, then I personally believe that makes you a witch, if you want to be called one. Certainly, it is still an emotive word for some, but I tend to think that it is their problem, not mine, and am happy to be labelled a witch, although it is uncommon within our tradition, despite both Odin and Thor seeking their aid within the mythology.

All this means that some of the hardest questions we have to answer about our beliefs come from ourselves, rather than from outside. How do we live ethically, on a day to day basis? Where does our respect for the law give way to our right of defence, and how do we interpret the ancient texts meanings in our personal lives? How do we label ourselves and regard the Gods and Goddesses, as spiritual beings or extensions of our own psyche? Living the Norse Tradition is much harder than reading about it!

A niding pole

Practical

1. Imagine a favourite aunt has written to you. She has heard that you have began to 'dabble in the occult' and are 'taking an unhealthy interest in Germany.' She is elderly, and occasionally goes to church. Compose a diplomatic, but honest letter to allay her fears.

2. Some towns have moots nowadays - Pagan discussion groups that meet in pubs or houses, with people of different paths attending. If you can get to one, how about getting a discussion going about our tradition, or an aspect of it? If they have lectures, maybe you could even offer to give a short talk. Be

ready to defend or explain your beliefs, without attacking the differing ideas of others.

Recommended Reading

Anon. translated G.N. Garmonsway - *The Anglo Saxon Chronicle* (Everyman)
Dorothy Whitelock - *The Beginnings of English Society* (Pelican)
Rudolph Simek trans. Angela Hall - *Dictionary of Northern Mythology* (D.S. Brewer)
John Yeowell - *Odinism & Christianity under the 3rd Reich* (Odinic Rite:Edda)
Bernard King - *Ultima Thule: The Vanished Northern Homeland* (Rune Gild UK)

Chapter 11

Where To Go From Here

If you have by now decided to follow a Northern Tradition path, you might be wondering how to progress from the end of this book. First and foremost, you will have to decide whether you wish to specialise in particular aspects. Do you want to explore the ways of the Anglo Saxons or Norse? Do you want to train to be a gothi/gytha priest/priestess role, or do you see yourself in a more shamanistic role, as a female volva or male shaman. Also, you must consider whether you want to dedicate yourself to one particular God or Goddess rather than a whole pantheon.

There are also the warrior cults to consider; The best known of these is the berserker, or bear shirt cult, whose adherents emulated a bear, and whipped themselves up into a fighting frenzy. Similar in nature are the Ulfhednar wolf warrior cult. There is also one brief reference to Chati, which seems to refer to warriors with a cat totem, and the Svinfylking who related closely to the sacred boar of Frey. (There are references to boar cults amongst both Saxons and Scandinavians, and at least two boars head helmets have been found in England.) Not much is known about the practices or rites of any of these warrior cults, but they may well be worth exploring if you are a fighter in spirit. The Saxon hero Hereward the Wake who fought a guerrilla war against the Normans is credited with killing a Norwegian bear, and called upon Danish berserkers with whom he had made friends to aid him in his fenland fight.

Boar's head helmet

Practical

1. Go out to a quiet natural place and meditate on what you have read in this book. Decide whether this path is for you, and if so, whether you want a specialised role within it. Decide to whether you identify especially with any particular deity. Make a personal oath about what you intend to do, and ask the help of all the Gods and Goddesses.

USEFUL ADDRESSES

You might like to try and contact others of our tradition to exchange ideas, join together in a hearth or be taught. Here are the addresses of some organisations to help you. In each case, send a stamped addressed envelope for your reply, or international reply coupons:

ODINSHOF, BM: Tercel, London,WC1N 3XX

RING OF TROTH UK, BM: Troth, London, WC1N 3XX

KITH OF YGGDRASIL, www.kith-of-yggdrasil.org

THE PAGAN FEDERATION, BM:7097, London, WC1N 3XX

The last of these is not an Odinist organisation, but provides information and contacts on all paths of Paganism for its members, and runs magazines, moots and conferences as well as publishing the Northern Tradition Information Pack. **Website** http://www.paganfed.org

There is a specialist Anglo Saxon historical society, who are not specifically heathen but are very helpful with all things of that era. In modern language they are known as the English Companions, but their proper title is:

Da Engliscan Gesidas, BM Box 4336, London, WC1N 3XX. They have a web site at:
http://www.kami.demon.co.uk/gesithas/

There is some interesting material too on:
http://www.asbooks.co.uk

http://www.astradyne.co.uk/midgard

PETE JENNINGS, BM: Gippeswic, London,WC1N 3XX. You may contact me at this address, but no replies will be issued without a stamped addressed envelope (UK) or two International Reply Coupons (Rest of world).You may also e mail me on pete@gippeswic.demon.co.uk or visit my web site (with lots of heathen links) at www.gippeswic.demon.co.uk

Elsewhere around the world, there are many more Asatru organisations and publishers, particularly in the USA. Inevitably, the list becomes out of date as soon as it is published, but this gives you a starting point to try and find others of a like mind. I cannot vouch for all that I have listed, as I do not know them personally. As always, when making new friends be careful, and do not be drawn into anything you are uncomfortable with. If you have access to the internet you can visit dozens of sites run by individual hearths as well as organisations. The biggest listing of links I have found is on the first site named here:

Irmisul Aettir http://www.irminsul.org

Ring Of Troth (USA) & **Idunna** magazine, PO Box 25637, Tempe, AZ 85285, USA http://www.thetroth.org

The Asatru Folk Assembly, PO Box 445, Nevada City, CA. 95959 USA

Asatru Alliance, *Vor Tru* magazine & World Tree Publications, PO Box 961, Payson, Az 85547, USA

The Rune Gild, PO Box 7622, University Station, Austin, TX 78713, USA   http://www.runegild.org

American Vinland Association, 537 Jones St. 2154, San Francisco,CA 94102 USA http://vinland.org/heathen/ava/
Hrafnar, C/ODiana Paxson Box 5521, Berkeley, CA94705,USA. http://vinland.org/heathen/hrafnar

Uncle Thors magazine, The Trollwise Press, PO Box 080437, Staten Island, NY 10308-0005, USA.

Eagles Reach/Aernfolk, c/o Ymir Thurnarsson, PO Box 327, Roanoke, TX 76262 USA. http://members.tripod. com/~aernfol/index-2html

Heritage & Tradition, CP 244, SUCC. P.A.T., Montreal, Quebec H1B 5K3 Canada

Bifrost Kindred, Suite 131, 5642-23 Ave, Edmonton, AB T6L 6NZ Canada http://www.geocities.com /Athens /Forum / 2716/

Icelandic Asatru Association, PO Box 1423, 123 Reykjavik, Iceland.

Renewal Magazine, PO Box 4333, University Of Melbourne, Victoria 3052, Australia,

Assembley Of Elder Troth,PO Box 331X, Leumah, NSW 2560, Australia,http://203.15.68.48/Pagan/AET.html

De Noordse Traditie, Postbus 1292, 2302, BG Leiden, Netherlands. http://www1.tip.nl/~t887876

Bifrost,Norway http://www.bifrost.no/enghome.html

Gladsaxe Blodtgilde, Trongaardsvej 44,2800 Lyngby, Danmark http://www.lyngbyes.dk

Sveriges Asatrosamfund, Box 4001, 13604 Haninge, Sweden TEL. 08 7412101 http://www.asatro.a.se/

Natveket For Nordisk Sed, Sweden, http://www.samfalligheten.org

Rabenclan, Germany http://www.rabenclan.de/

Organise Your Own Hearth

If you cannot find an existing hearth group to join in your area it can be rewarding to organise several beginners to meet and learn together sometimes, rather than relying on an 'expert' to teach you. After all, our tradition teaches us to be self sufficient and independent. Both Odinshof and Ring of Troth can advise you on how best to do this, and provide you with correspondence course training and contacts in your area that may be potential recruits. My advice is to start small and look for some practical commitment to the path in those who seek to join. It is better to have a small dedicated hearth than a large one with a floating population of people all with separate agendas.

Agree a written set of ground rules and objectives at the start, so people know where they stand. Now that you have made some decisions about how you plan to continue, you may well want to go back to the recommended reading from the different chapters to learn about specific topics relative to the path you have chosen.

Remember though that there is a limit to how much one can learn from books. At some stage one must actually do things and learn from the experience! I will however finish with a couple of fictional books that did not fit into any particular chapter, but are worth reading anyway, and wish you an interesting and rewarding quest.

Recommended Reading

J.R.R. Tolkien - *Lord of the Rings* (Harper Collins)
Brian Bates - *The Way of the Wyrd* (Arrow)

Norse Tradition books from Capall Bann

Asyniur - Women's Mysteries in the Northern Tradition
Sheena McGrath
"excellent. Well researched and well balanced...scrupulous honesty...she is clearly a writer to watch out for in future...highly recommended" White Dragon
Unlike other titles in this area, this book looks at all aspects of women's lives, their magic and their religion in the Northern Tradition. Topics covered include the nature of women's activities from the 'traditional' position of housewife to those of scald and warrior, the role of female figures in creation and Ragnarok myths, a comprehensive coverage of Northern Tradition Goddesses, rituals specific to women, runes and the female power of foreseeing events, Seidr - the combination of witchcraft and shamanism, its connections with Freya as well as the connections between her, fertility magic and Seidr itself.   ISBN 186163 004 2   £10.95

The Mysteries of the Runes   Michael Howard
A full investigation into rune origins, symbolism & use, traced from Neolithic & Bronze Age symbols & their connection with other magical & mystical symbols. Runic divination by Germanic tribes, Saxons and Vikings are also covered. Odin is discussed, as the shaman-god of the runes, with his myths & legends, the Wild Hunt, and the Valkyries. Magical uses of runes are explored with their use in divination. Fascinating information is included on discoveries made in archaeological excavations, rune masters & mistresses, the bog sacrifices of Scandinavia & rune master training. Runic symbolism is detailed together with descriptions of each of the eight runes of Freya's, Haegl's & Tyr's Aetts with divinity, religious symbolism & spiritual meanings based on The Anglo Saxon Rune Poem. How to make your own set of runes, how to cast them for divination with suggested layouts & the use of rune magic. Also covers the gods & goddesses of the Aesir & Vanir, their myths & legends & the seasonal cycle of Northern Tradition festivals. Other topics covered include Hyperborea & the 'Atlantis of the North', duality in Indo-European religion, the Web of Wyrd & the Norns, Saxon/Norse paganism & traditional witchcraft. ISBN 189830 707 5   £9.95   Illustrated

Runic Astrology Nigel Pennick
Specialisation and new technology have led us to become fragmented in our perception, seeing the parts and not the whole. We are alienated from the natural time cycles of the seasons and the stars and have lost track of our place in the universe. Runic Astrology sets out to remedy this malaise. The Runes are ancient, based in nature, related to archetypal forces and to the natural cycles once followed by our pagan ancestors and celebrated in such festivals as Beltane and Samhain; festivals still preserved in part, in the Church calender. Nigel is a persuasive advocate of a new way of approaching the modern world. He discusses the place of the runes in the Northern Tradition, looking at its attitude to destiny and free will and relating its cosmology to modern physics. The author discusses the origins of the runes as well as the esoteric numerological significance of traditional divisions of time, space and money. The significance of the planets and fixed stars in the Northern Tradition is described and the runic birthchart explored. Runic cycles, biorythms, weather cycles, even stock market cycles, all are discussed and contribute to the unique character of the book. ISBN 1898307 45 8   £10.95   Illustrated

The Inner Mysteries of the Goths   Nigel Pennick

"A necessary addition to one's library" Odinism Today
A book about the runes used by the ancient Goths, & their unique rune-derived alphabet, also used as a divination system. The runes have developed & continue to flourish, entering new areas unheard of by their practitioners of ancient days. Now, in this book, published 1400 years after the Roman Catholic church suppressed the Gothic Alphabet, the Gothic staves are described again together with their runic siblings as a system of seership. With the Gothic alphabet, each character possessed an individual meaning that emanated partly from the spirit of the age, partly from the conscious & subconscious of the alphabets' creator and partly from the undefinable realm of spirit. Gothic divination has no overall ruling text, only individual meanings & associations without giving a fixed, textual, association. It is up to us to use the power of divination wisely, for the good of all.   ISBN 1898307 45 8   £10.95   illustrated

Rune Rede, Wisdom and Magic for the Life Journey

Ruarik Grimnisson
This book has been written in answer to the increased demand for 'traditional' Rune Lore. It is the product of 10 years of research and practical experimentation. This book incorporates the essentials that are common to those cultures where Runes were used, and remains true to their Heathen origins. The ways of Rune working have evolved over centuries but the essential symbolism, as a key to understanding the profound mysteries of existence, is just as relevant today, as it was to our ancestors. The Runic 'alphabets' were not just a system of writing for the Germanic peoples - they were a Life-Code. Encrypted in their numerical ordering and individual symbolism is a guide to the life journey of the soul - a holistic approach for the individual and collective folk to survive and thrive in the worlds of nature, mankind and the spiritual realms. Their magick arose from the understanding of the inseparability of all phenomena - what our ancestors called the Wyrd. This book presents an integrated collection of basic Rune Lore in the manner the author believes it was meant to be given - as a counsel for the soul's life journey. The Old English word for counsel is "Red"- Rede, hence the title of this book. The author has used the collective system of the twenty four rune staves known as the "Elder Futhark", they being the oldest complete runic system yet found. This book contains the codes that will make the way clear. It has been designed as a 'ready reference', not only for all who wish to explore the patterns of Wyrd, but for those who seek essential reference to the power of the Runes, manifested and un-manifested. For those who are seeking insight into the psychological world of our pre-industrial ancestors, this book will reveal to you their basic attitudes and expectations. The ancestral mythology interwoven with each rune-rede is presented for your own contemplation. Study of the knowledge herein seen through the lens of heathen understanding will reveal an alternative map of reality that will aid you on your life journey. For the student of the Occult, it will serve as a stimulation for deeper mystical studies.
ISBN 186163 126X   £14.95   illustrated

Beyond the Yew Dale   Paul Sykes

This book explores Nordic Mythology and its influence on the interpretation of runes when used for divination. The text includes original material on Rune casts and refines some earlier ideas on spreads and casts from other sources, and is backed up by detailed imaginative drawings for each rune. Thus giving the reader a pictorial as well as textual viewpoint to work from. A simple yet informative book, Beyond the Yew Dale provides an excellent introduction to the subjects of divination and mythology for beginners. It is also a comprehensive guide for those already familiar with the topic.   ISBN 186163 1839   illustrated

FREE DETAILED CATALOGUE

Capall Bann is owned and run by people actively involved in many of the areas in which we publish. A detailed illustrated catalogue is available on request, SAE or International Postal Coupon appreciated. **Titles can be ordered direct from Capall Bann, post free in the UK** (cheque or PO with order) or from good bookshops and specialist outlets.

Do contact us for details on the latest releases at: **Capall Bann Publishing, Auton Farm, Milverton, Somerset, TA4 1NE.** Titles include:

A Breath Behind Time, Terri Hector
Angels and Goddesses - Celtic Christianity & Paganism, M. Howard
Arthur - The Legend Unveiled, C Johnson & E Lung
Astrology The Inner Eye - A Guide in Everyday Language, E Smith
Auguries and Omens - The Magical Lore of Birds, Yvonne Aburrow
Asyniur - Womens Mysteries in the Northern Tradition, S McGrath
Beginnings - Geomancy, Builder's Rites & Electional Astrology in the
    European Tradition, Nigel Pennick
Between Earth and Sky, Julia Day
Book of the Veil , Peter Paddon
Caer Sidhe - Celtic Astrology and Astronomy, Vol 1, Michael Bayley
Caer Sidhe - Celtic Astrology and Astronomy, Vol 2 M Bayley
Call of the Horned Piper, Nigel Jackson
Cat's Company, Ann Walker
Celtic Faery Shamanism, Catrin James
Celtic Faery Shamanism - The Wisdom of the Otherworld, Catrin James
Celtic Lore & Druidic Ritual, Rhiannon Ryall
Celtic Sacrifice - Pre Christian Ritual & Religion, Marion Pearce
Celtic Saints and the Glastonbury Zodiac, Mary Caine
Circle and the Square, Jack Gale
Compleat Vampyre - The Vampyre Shaman, Nigel Jackson
Creating Form From the Mist - The Wisdom of Women in Celtic Myth and
    Culture, Lynne Sinclair-Wood
Crystal Clear - A Guide to Quartz Crystal, Jennifer Dent
Crystal Doorways, Simon & Sue Lilly
Crossing the Borderlines - Guising, Masking & Ritual Animal Disguise in the
    European Tradition, Nigel Pennick
Dragons of the West, Nigel Pennick
Earth Dance - A Year of Pagan Rituals, Jan Brodie

Earth Harmony - Places of Power, Holiness & Healing, Nigel Pennick
Earth Magic, Margaret McArthur
Eildon Tree (The) Romany Language & Lore, Michael Hoadley
Enchanted Forest - The Magical Lore of Trees, Yvonne Aburrow
Eternal Priestess, Sage Weston
Eternally Yours Faithfully, Roy Radford & Evelyn Gregory
Everything You Always Wanted To Know About Your Body, But So Far
    Nobody's Been Able To Tell You, Chris Thomas & D Baker
Face of the Deep - Healing Body & Soul, Penny Allen
Fairies in the Irish Tradition, Molly Gowen
Familiars - Animal Powers of Britain, Anna Franklin
Fool's First Steps, (The) Chris Thomas
Forest Paths - Tree Divination, Brian Harrison, Ill. S. Rouse
From Past to Future Life, Dr Roger Webber
Gardening For Wildlife Ron Wilson
God Year, The, Nigel Pennick & Helen Field
Goddess on the Cross, Dr George Young
Goddess Year, The, Nigel Pennick & Helen Field
Goddesses, Guardians & Groves, Jack Gale
Handbook For Pagan Healers, Liz Joan
Handbook of Fairies, Ronan Coghlan
Healing Book, The, Chris Thomas and Diane Baker
Healing Homes, Jennifer Dent
Healing Journeys, Paul Williamson
Healing Stones, Sue Philips
Herb Craft - Shamanic & Ritual Use of Herbs, Lavender & Franklin
Hidden Heritage - Exploring Ancient Essex, Terry Johnson
Hub of the Wheel, Skytoucher
In Search of Herne the Hunter, Eric Fitch
Inner Celtia, Alan Richardson & David Annwn
Inner Mysteries of the Goths, Nigel Pennick
Inner Space Workbook - Develop Thru Tarot, C Summers & J Vayne
Intuitive Journey, Ann Walker Isis - African Queen, Akkadia Ford
Journey Home, The, Chris Thomas
Kecks, Keddles & Kesh - Celtic Lang & The Cog Almanac, Bayley
Language of the Psycards, Berenice
Legend of Robin Hood, The, Richard Rutherford-Moore
Lid Off the Cauldron, Patricia Crowther
Light From the Shadows - Modern Traditional Witchcraft, Gwyn
Living Tarot, Ann Walker
Lore of the Sacred Horse, Marion Davies
Lost Lands & Sunken Cities (2nd ed.), Nigel Pennick
Magic of Herbs - A Complete Home Herbal, Rhiannon Ryall
Magical Guardians - Exploring the Spirit and Nature of Trees, Philip Heselton
Magical History of the Horse, Janet Farrar & Virginia Russell
Magical Lore of Animals, Yvonne Aburrow

Magical Lore of Cats, Marion Davies
Magical Lore of Herbs, Marion Davies
Magick Without Peers, Ariadne Rainbird & David Rankine
Masks of Misrule - Horned God & His Cult in Europe, Nigel Jackson
Medicine For The Coming Age, Lisa Sand MD
Medium Rare - Reminiscences of a Clairvoyant, Muriel Renard
Menopausal Woman on the Run, Jaki da Costa
Mind Massage - 60 Creative Visualisations, Marlene Maundrill
Mirrors of Magic - Evoking the Spirit of the Dewponds, P Heselton
Moon Mysteries, Jan Brodie
Mysteries of the Runes, Michael Howard
Mystic Life of Animals, Ann Walker
New Celtic Oracle The, Nigel Pennick & Nigel Jackson
Oracle of Geomancy, Nigel Pennick
Pagan Feasts - Seasonal Food for the 8 Festivals, Franklin & Phillips
Patchwork of Magic - Living in a Pagan World, Julia Day
Pathworking - A Practical Book of Guided Meditations, Pete Jennings
Personal Power, Anna Franklin
Pickingill Papers - The Origins of Gardnerian Wicca, Bill Liddell
Pillars of Tubal Cain, Nigel Jackson
Places of Pilgrimage and Healing, Adrian Cooper
Practical Divining, Richard Foord
Practical Meditation, Steve Hounsome
Practical Spirituality, Steve Hounsome
Psychic Self Defence - Real Solutions, Jan Brodie
Real Fairies, David Tame
Reality - How It Works & Why It Mostly Doesn't, Rik Dent
Romany Tapestry, Michael Houghton
Runic Astrology, Nigel Pennick
Sacred Animals, Gordon MacLellan
Sacred Celtic Animals, Marion Davies, Ill. Simon Rouse
Sacred Dorset - On the Path of the Dragon, Peter Knight
Sacred Grove - The Mysteries of the Forest, Yvonne Aburrow
Sacred Geometry, Nigel Pennick
Sacred Nature, Ancient Wisdom & Modern Meanings, A Cooper
Sacred Ring - Pagan Origins of British Folk Festivals, M. Howard
Season of Sorcery - On Becoming a Wisewoman, Poppy Palin
Seasonal Magic - Diary of a Village Witch, Paddy Slade
Secret Places of the Goddess, Philip Heselton
Secret Signs & Sigils, Nigel Pennick
Self Enlightenment, Mayan O'Brien
Spirits of the Air, Jaq D Hawkins
Spirits of the Earth, Jaq D Hawkins
Spirits of the Earth, Jaq D Hawkins
Stony Gaze, Investigating Celtic Heads John Billingsley
Stumbling Through the Undergrowth , Mark Kirwan-Heyhoe

Subterranean Kingdom, The, revised 2nd ed, Nigel Pennick
Symbols of Ancient Gods, Rhiannon Ryall
Talking to the Earth, Gordon MacLellan
Taming the Wolf - Full Moon Meditations, Steve Hounsome
Teachings of the Wisewomen, Rhiannon Ryall
The Other Kingdoms Speak, Helena Hawley
Tree: Essence of Healing, Simon & Sue Lilly
Tree: Essence, Spirit & Teacher, Simon & Sue Lilly
Through the Veil, Peter Paddon
Torch and the Spear, Patrick Regan
Understanding Chaos Magic, Jaq D Hawkins
Vortex - The End of History, Mary Russell
Warp and Weft - In Search of the I-Ching, William de Fancourt
Warriors at the Edge of Time, Jan Fry
Water Witches, Tony Steele
Way of the Magus, Michael Howard
Weaving a Web of Magic, Rhiannon Ryall
West Country Wicca, Rhiannon Ryall
Wildwitch - The Craft of the Natural Psychic, Poppy Palin
Wildwood King , Philip Kane
Witches of Oz, Matthew & Julia Philips
Wondrous Land - The Faery Faith of Ireland by Dr Kay Mullin
Working With the Merlin, Geoff Hughes
Your Talking Pet, Ann Walker

FREE detailed catalogue and FREE 'Inspiration' magazine

Contact: Capall Bann Publishing, Auton Farm, Milverton, Somerset, TA4 1NE